NEW TESTAMENT MESSAGE

A Biblical-Theological Commentary

Wilfrid Harrington, O.P. and Donald Senior, C.P.
EDITORS

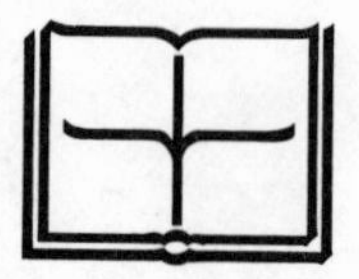

New Testament Message, Volume 8

THE ACTS

Jerome Crowe, C.P.

Michael Glazier, Inc.
Wilmington, Delaware

MICHAEL GLAZIER, INC.
1210A King Street
Wilmington, Delaware 19801

Library of Congress Catalog Card Number: 79-53890
International Standard Book Number
New Testament Message series: 0-89453-123-9
ACTS: 0-89453-131-X

Printed in the United States of America by Abbey Press

Contents

Editors' Preface vii
Introduction to the Commentary ix
Luke's Introduction: The Change of Eras
— 1:1-11 xxiii

PART I WITNESSES IN JERUSALEM
— 1:12-5:42 1
The Restoration of the Twelve—1:12-26 3
Pentecost—2:1-40 8
The Community Created by the Spirit
—2:41-5:42 17

PART II JUDEA AND SAMARIA—6:1-12:25 37
Stephen—6:1-8:3 39
Philip, Peter and John—8:4-40 52
Saul—9:1-31 61
Peter—9:32-11:18 69
Antioch and Jerusalem—11:19-12:25 82

PART III "TO THE ENDS OF THE EARTH"
—13:1-28:31 93
Missions of Paul and Barnabas—13:1-15:35 95
Missions of Paul—15:36-21:14 120
From Jerusalem to Rome—21:15-28:31 160

Further Reading 201

EDITORS' PREFACE

New Testament Message is a commentary series designed to bring the best of biblical scholarship to a wide audience. Anyone who is sensitive to the mood of the church today is aware of a deep craving for the Word of God. This interest in reading and praying the scriptures is not confined to a religious elite. The desire to strengthen one's faith and to mature in prayer has brought Christians of all types and all ages to discover the beauty of the biblical message. Our age has also been heir to an avalanche of biblical scholarship. Recent archaeological finds, new manuscript evidence, and the increasing volume of specialized studies on the Bible have made possible a much more profound penetration of the biblical message. But the flood of information and its technical nature keeps much of this scholarship out of the hands of the Christian who is eager to learn but is not a specialist. *New Testament Message* is a response to this need.

The subtitle of the series is significant: "A Biblical-Theological Commentary." Each volume in the series, while drawing on up-to-date scholarship, concentrates on bringing to the fore in understandable terms the specific message of each biblical author. The essay-format (rather than a word-by-word commentary) helps the reader savor the beauty and power of the biblical message and, at the same time, understand the sensitive task of responsible biblical interpretation.

A distinctive feature of the series is the amount of space given to the "neglected" New Testament writings, such as Colossians, James, Jude, the Pastoral Letters, the Letters of Peter and John. These briefer biblical books make a significant but often overlooked contribution to the richness of the New Testament. By assigning larger than normal coverage to these books, the series hopes to give these parts of Scripture the attention they deserve.

Because *New Testament Message* is aimed at the entire English speaking world, it is a collaborative effort of international proportions. The twenty-two contributors represent biblical scholarship in North America, Ireland, Britain and Australia. Each of the contributors is a recognized expert in his or her field, has published widely, and has been chosen because of a proven ability to communicate at a popular level. And, while all of the contributors are Roman Catholic, their work is addressed to the Christian community as a whole. The New Testament is the patrimony of all Christians. It is the hope of all concerned with this series that it will bring a fuller appreciation of God's saving Word to his people.

Wilfrid Harrington, O.P.
Donald Senior, C.P.

Introduction

1) A Second Volume

"In the first book . . .". Luke's opening words call the attention of the reader to the most basic principle in understanding the Acts of the Apostles. Acts does not stand on its own. It is the second of two volumes which together make one book. It presupposes a first volume, the Gospel of Luke.

Other Gospels tell the story of Jesus and conclude with the Resurrection. For all that Luke's Gospel runs parallel to them it has a purpose which they do not; it also functions as a preparation for Acts. To commence reading the story with Acts is like entering a two-part movie after intermission. The second volume does occasionally offer brief synopses of the first, as in the summaries of the life, death and resurrection of Jesus in the discourses of Peter and Paul; but the action has already begun in the first volume, the pattern of the action has already been established, the figures who bulk so large in the opening chapters of the second volume have already been on-stage for almost the whole of the first.

The first volume is deliberately incomplete, as if it were a preview of things to come in the second. At its beginning the prophet Simeon acclaims the new-born Jesus as "a light for the revelation of the Gentiles." Later John the Baptist proclaims that through the coming of Jesus "all men shall see the salvation of God," but even at its close the Good News of God's salvation has been proclaimed only on Jewish soil and Jesus himself has not personally encountered more than a handful of Gentiles.

The unity of the two volumes is underlined by the parallelism of their structure. The life of Jesus in the first volume falls into two main sections, his ministry in Galilee centring on the Twelve which concludes with his sending them out on mission, and the journey of Jesus to Jerusalem. The second volume also falls into two main sections, the first centring mainly on Jerusalem, Peter and the apostles, the second centred on Paul, turned towards Rome and concluding with Paul's journey. Some have found in the opening chapters of Acts a story of the infancy of the Church comparable to the infancy of Jesus in the Gospel. The parallelism of the two volumes can be elaborated in considerable detail; it provides a significant indication of the unity between them and Luke's intention in the whole book.

The story told in the second volume actually dictated not only the overall structure of the first but many of its details. The characteristic Lucan portrait of Jesus is painted in such a way as to show a continuity between Jesus and the Church. Luke underlines, in ways Mark and Matthew do not, the constant guidance of the Holy Spirit in the ministry of Jesus to prepare for the Pentecostal coming of the Spirit who will be the power and guide of the Church. Luke's emphasis on the prayer of Jesus shows where the prayer of the Church originates. Even such details as an insistence on Jesus' custom of preaching in the synagogue serves to show in his life the precedent and model of the early missioners.

Luke has devoted similar care to the details concerning "The Twelve" in the life of Jesus. In a number of details in which, again, he differs from Mark and Matthew, he shows Jesus associating the Twelve with him in his ministry, sending them out to preach, giving them authority over the new Israel. All this the first volume reveals and all this is presupposed by the second. An understanding of the second volume calls for constant reference to the first.

2) A Story

The one book has the same purpose in each of its volumes. Acts is as much "Gospel" as the first, not because it conforms to the literary form already set by Mark, but because it communicates the same Good News of God's salvation. The Good News can be communicated in many forms of writing, as the range of books of the New Testament illustrates; but whereas in the first volume Luke followed the precedent set by Mark in telling the story of the life, death and resurrection of Jesus, he alone chose to communicate the Good News by continuing with the story of the early decades of the Church. Just as Mark before him collected anecdotes, sayings and stories and made of them a connected story of the life of Jesus, so Luke draws on comparable material to tell the story of the early Church.

Acts is a "story," a connected narrative of events involving movement, conflict, change. It includes the lesser "stories" of many individuals and groups; Luke connects them into a pattern which constitutes the larger story. This offers him the possibility of using material of many kinds. There are samples of reasoned argument comparable to the epistles of Paul in a series of discourses (though much of these speeches, too, is a recitation of the "story" of God's great acts in the past) which draw on the Scriptures to prove that Jesus is the Messiah. There are a series of anecdotes, stories of miraculous cures and exorcisms comparable in form to the stories of the first volume and each, like them, "the Gospel in miniature." There are stories of conversions, accounts of journeys and the foundation of the early communities, samples of the early Church's prayer and the utterances of its prophets.

It is well to attend the "story" character of Acts to avoid common misunderstandings. Luke has an excellent claim to the title of historian, but he is primarily engaged in telling a "story." It is through the literary medium of the story that he communicates. In the studied devices or individual literary instinct that highlights the elements of a scene or dialogue, in the simplification that eliminates details distracting from the central issues and emphasizing what lies at its heart, in irony, pathos, suspense, in all that opens the reader's eyes to the wonder of the era of the Spirit, "the total dispossession of Satan and the ultimate omnipotence of God's grace" - in these and other ways in which he tells his "story" Luke is communicating the Good News.

The common comparison of Luke with the artist or the dramatist simply illustrates this "story" character in other ways. Many have been impressed by the pictorial effect he creates, his ability to compose a scene, to convey the Good News through a series of tableaux, like a painter, concerned not so much to capture what offers itself to the sight of men with photographic accuracy but to communicate an insight into the mystery of human life by colour, light, shade and the composition of a scene. Like the dramatist or playwright Luke communicates with his contemporary audience by means of the action onstage, where the story of the past provokes responses to life in the circumstances of their own present.

In all that moves the reader to identify with one or other character, to recognise his or her story in the story onstage, to a clearer insight into life in the Christian community in this present world, Luke communicates the Good News. If he tells the "story" of Peter and John and the apostles, of Stephen and the Hellenists, of Philip and Barnabas and Paul, he does not do it with a meticulous quest for accuracy in details of time or place or costume or chronological sequence, but with the instinct of the artist or dramatist to communicate with his audience at the level of their deepest attitudes to life in their world and their commitment to the very task he is himself engaged in, the communication of the Good News to others.

3) Retrospect

Luke believed that the Church in which his audience lived had originated by a process of organic growth from Jesus and the men and women associated with him during his life. He also believed that growth was directed by the Holy Spirit, almost by definition "the surprise of God," so that it had come in paradoxical ways, but he saw an underlying continuity between the life of Jesus and the life of the Church. The passage of time had revealed a significance in the events of the past that had often gone by unnoticed by those who participated in them. It was not given to everyone to discern immediately the paradoxical action of the Spirit. Later developments clarified the ambiguity of earlier episodes, especially those that were disconcerting, painful, even shocking. Just as the two disciples were saddened and perplexed at the apparent shattering of their hopes by the death of Jesus until enlightened by the risen Lord on the road to Emmaus, so later disciples struggled to understand the hostility they encountered from Judaism and the outbreak of persecution.

Their enlightenment by the Holy Spirit came only gradually. It is doubtful if traditional, conservative Jewish members of the Jerusalem community were able to perceive in the iconoclasm of the radical Stephen what Luke shows him to have been, "a man of grace and power." The admission of the Gentiles to the community caused by major crisis of identity that lasted for over a decade; the enlightenment of the Holy Spirit came only through an extended period of debate among people of very diverse mentalities before its final resolution.

Luke enjoys the benefit of retrospect. He benefits from the "contemplation and study" of five decades of believers, from "the intimate understanding of spiritual things" they have experienced. His portrait colours the events of the past with the significance time has revealed in them. His drama communicates the insight that decades of "the practise and life of the believing and praying Church" have discovered.

4) Theophilus

The audience Luke addressed, however, seemed far removed from its origins. It was separated by more than half a century from Jesus and the first Jerusalem community, by two decades from the apostle Paul whose missionary activity exemplified so well its own mushroom growth and spread into the Gentile world. Christians then might well have been prone to comparisons quite as rueful as any later generations have made between the contemporary Church and the simplicities of the life of Jesus.

Fifty years ago Jesus and his companions were proclaiming God's imminent Kingdom to Jews in Palestine; Theophilus was acquainted with predominantly Gentile communities spread throughout the Roman empire. The Jewish world of Jesus and the Jerusalem community was dead and gone; nothing symbolised its passing with more brutal clarity than the destruction of Jerusalem and the Temple in which they had gathered for prayer. Now was "the time of the Gentiles." But even Gentile Christians of his father's generation had spent their lives in eager expectation of the glorious return of Jesus. For men of his generation the decades had rolled relentlessly on; apocalyptic expectation had to give way to the realities of life in this continuing world. Who knew how long it might continue - a century?... perhaps even a millennium?

5) A History

Men who live in imminent expectation of the Parousia do not write the story of the past - after all, to whom would they bequeath it? By writing his story Luke shows that he is taking the present seriously and that he expects his work to be of value in the future. The simple fact of writing his second volume shows that Luke regarded the events of the early Church as valuable in themselves; the story of the early Church, like the words and deeds of Jesus, is revelatory of God's purpose. To insist that Acts is to be considered first of all as a "story" is not to assert that it is a fairy story. Paul, telling his own story to King Agrippa, could say that "this was not done in a corner" and the whole of Acts concerns real persons, real interactions and conflicts that happened on a public stage.

Luke is the first "historian" of the Church. The introduction of his first volume aligns him with historians of his era like Livy, Flavius Josephus and Tacitus, who wrote within a tradition of history established by Herodotus and Thucydides five centuries before. Luke has done his research and he intends to write "an orderly account." Like them he sets out to present a pattern in the succession of events; but whereas the pattern they sought to establish arose out of the interplay of the human decisions of great men with a rather nebulous "fate," Luke offers an insight into the "plan" or "will" of the one true God offering salvation to all people.

Luke used sources, both oral and written. Scholars are divided in their estimates as to the extent of these sources, their nature, and the way Luke used them. In the first volume his story can be checked against his sources by simply comparing his Gospel with Mark's in material they have in common. In Acts the sources he used are no longer extant and have to be reconstructed, generally from the text of Acts itself. The reason for divergent estimates lies in Luke's artistic and dramatic skill, in his ability to integrate pieces of different provenance into a mosaic spanning three decades in time and all the distance between Jerusalem and Rome.

It is very likely that he drew on an itinerary that provided detailed information on the second and third missionary journey. The most natural explanation of the "We-Passages" (16:10-17;20:5-15;21:1-18;27:1 - 28:16) is that they are excerpts from the journal of someone who travelled with Paul and in fact of Luke himself. It is likely that he used the records as well as the reminiscences of the community at Antioch and that some such recollections are at the basis of his presentation of the community in Jerusalem.

While Acts cannot be checked against its sources it can be checked against information from other sources, Jewish writings such as those of Qumran, the historian Josephus, Jewish legal procedure known from the writings of a somewhat later age, and Christian writings such as those of Paul, particularly valuable for that section of the story that concerns his conversion, his dealings with the apostles in

Jerusalem, and his missionary journeys. Profane sources testify to Luke's accuracy in what concerns titles of Roman officials, law and procedure.

This commentary occasionally remarks on the factual or historical value of sections of Acts. It enquires, that is, into the "history" of Peter or the primitive Church. That enquiry is entirely legitimate and necessary, but our main concern remains Luke's "story."

6) Discourses

A major feature of the histories of Herodotus, Thucydides and their successors were the discourses they placed in the mouths of their subjects. They disclaim any intention to reproduce verbatim the words of the speakers; a discourse Tacitus attributes to Claudius can be compared with the original discourse which is known and differs considerably from it. While they do claim to reproduce the general tenour of the original address, it can be shown that they really make use of the discourse as a literary device to transmit their own ideas.

The discourses in Acts were even more important to Luke. This can be seen from the amount of space he devotes to them. At least a quarter of the book's one thousand verses consists of discourse. If the settings in which the discourses are placed are added, the proportion exceeds one half.

These discourses are commonly numbered at twenty four. They vary considerably. The variety can be seen first in the range of speakers, who number seven and range from Peter and Paul through Gamaliel, Stephen and James, to Demetrius the silversmith and the town clerk of Ephesus, Tertullus the Jewish advocate and Festus, the Roman governor. They differ also in literary form; Peter alone delivers discourses that can be classified as missionary, apologetic and ecclesial and to these can be added a farewell discourse of Paul as well as various exhortations and judicial harangues. Finally they are addressed to different audiences: Christian, Jewish and pagan. All these factors are important in assessing their place in Luke's book.

For it was to take their place in Luke's story that they were composed. Though brief they are finished products in their own right and not summaries of longer discourses. They are aimed at the reader, as can be seen where the speaker either presupposes information that the reader has but his audience has not, or where the speaker imports information superfluous to his audience but necessary to the reader. It can also be seen in those passages where the Jewish speaker addressing a Jewish audience bases his argument on the Greek translation of the Scriptures familiar to the reader at the very points where it differs from the Hebrew original with which the speaker's audience might be supposed to be familiar.

On the other hand Luke utilises in the discourses themes as old as the preaching of the apostles which the discourses purport to convey and he is using the favourite Scripture texts of the early community to prove the Messiahship of Jesus. At times, too, viewpoints are expressed in the discourses which are at variance with what we know to be characteristic of Luke. This can be taken as a sign of respect for older formulations of the faith which he respects and reports but does not find helpful for his own audience.

7) Theology

But the final product is stamped with Luke's distinctive language and style and cast in the mould of his own favourite categories and conceptions. It is "the teaching of the "apostles" that he communicates, but in his own way and for his own audience. It is the one Gospel of Jesus Christ he communicates, but it is the Gospel according to Luke.

What is Luke's "distinctive mould"? What kind of "pattern" does his characteristic insight discern in the events he narrates? To ask these questions is to pose the question of the theology of Luke. One might ask what kind of "theology" can be derived from a work like this; for if Luke specialises in theology by tableaux, one will approach with caution the work of reducing those scenes to the limits of a conceptual system. Conceptual analysis and systematization of a work of this kind is likely to leave a residue unaccounted for, a residue which consists of precisely the elements that effect the miraculous mutation of "theology" into "The Good News of Our Lord Jesus Christ."

The distinctive pattern Luke sees in the events of his history is revealed in the discourse of Gamaliel. "If this plan or undertaking is of men, it will fail; but if it is of God, you will not be able to overthrow them" (5:38-39). Underlying or pervading and directing all the events is the "plan" or active "will" of God.

The implementation of that plan, it is clear, began well before the beginning of Acts. Luke's first volume has already shown how God's plan spans and unifies the time of Israel, the time of Jesus, and the time of the Church. Indeed, since it is aimed at the salvation of all people that action will have been operative in the affairs of men since the creation of Adam. It is the plan "served by David in his generation" (13:22,36) that was made known to Paul on the Damascus road (22:14) so that he could declare it, in all its final clarity, to others (20:27).

Since it is God's plan it "must" be fulfilled. In inspiring the utterances of psalmist and prophet, God outlined in the Scriptures the things that "had to be fulfilled." These things embrace, centrally, the mystery of the death and resurrection of Christ, for the Scriptures show that "the Messiah had to suffer and to rise from the dead" (17:3); his death, however scandalous, was still "according to the definite plan and foreknowledge of God" (2:23). But this divine "must" extends to other details of the life of the community, from items that seem as diverse as the apostasy of Judas and his replacement by Matthias (1:16,21), to the sufferings of Paul and persecution of the Church (9:16; 14:22) and finally to his journey back to Jerusalem and thence to Rome (19:21).

Against this divine plan no human counsels (27:12,42) or plots (9:24;20:3,19) can possibly prevail, even when they seem to dictate the immediate course of events, for all is subservient to God's design. Similarly, the real turning points in the story are not human decisions or heroic acts but initiatives of God, often through visions, dreams, prophecies and manifest if unexplained divine interventions.

God's "plan" is brought into effect by His "word," which He sent finally to Israel in the "good news of peace" proclaimed by Jesus (10:36). More than thirty times in Acts we read of "the word of God" (cf. 4:31;6:2) or "the word of the Lord" (cf. 8:25); or quite simply "the word" (cf. 4:4;6:4). When this is described as "the word of salvation" (cf. 13:26) or "the word of his grace" (14:3), we are not being informed of the content of God's message; "salvation" and "grace" are not the topics dealt with in the proclamation of the apostles - they are what *happens* in the proclamation of the apostles. In the preaching and mission of the Church God acts personally, salvation and grace become a present reality. So real is this conception of the active will of God at work in the mission of the church that "the word" is personified (6:7; 12:24; 19:20). Like Jesus (Lk 2:40) the word of God "grows" when apostles call men to repentance and they respond in faith and baptism.

Acts begins with the departure of the risen Jesus from the world in which his disciples are to live. Not only is the principal actor of the first volume offstage for the whole of the second, but Luke insists that this is a necessary part of God's plan. If it was necessary for the Messiah to suffer and thus enter his glory, it is equally necessary that "heaven receive him" until the time established by God (3:21). Is Jesus, then, an absentee Lord until the Parousia? If not, how is he present in and to his Church?

Earlier generations had bequeathed to Luke a whole litany of names or titles drawn from the Scriptures in which they had articulated their belief in the continuing active presence of Jesus. When he calls Jesus "Lord" he is using the terms of the earliest profession of Christian faith. When he outlines the preaching of the apostles he consistently calls Jesus "the Christ" (cf. 2:36; 9:22; 18:5,28), though he does not detail what his status as Messiah implies. Again the risen Jesus is the glorified Servant of Yahweh (3:13,14,26), the prophet like Moses "raised up" by God (3:22-33) who must be heard under penalty of exclusion from God's people, the "leader" and "Saviour," "ruler and deliverer" like Moses (5:31; 7:35).

Simply to list these titles does not show us how Luke saw the work of Jesus. They are often evocative rather than explanatory. When Luke falls back on them he is sometimes repeating terms from a litany dear to earlier Christians, as when he has Stephen refer to "the son of Man" (7:56), a title that had fallen into disuse well before his time. On the other hand it can be seen that the admission of pagans has revealed a greater depth in the title "Lord" than had been appreciated before, since it shows that he is sovereign master of all people (10:36). Is it possible to be more precise as to how Luke saw Jesus? For a start it must be said that it is to the Resurrection that Luke ascribes the new status of Jesus as Lord and Christ. Luke does not explore the saving value of the death of Jesus in the way Paul had done. In this he departs from many of his predecessors who had insisted that Christ died "for us" or "for our sins." Luke connects salvation, the pardon of sins, access to life, the gift of the Spirit of the Risen Jesus. Nor does he, like John, think of Jesus as a pre-existent divine being. For Luke Jesus becomes Son of God, and he does so in the Resurrection. It was in the raising him from the dead that God said "Thou art my Son, this day I have begotten thee" (Ps 2:7 cf. Acts 13:32-33). It is by raising Jesus from the dead that God "gives him a name," establishes him as unique source of God's saving power so that "there is no other name under heaven given among men by which we must be saved" (4:12).

In a number of ways Luke's story shows the presence of Christ becoming real in the ministry and life of the Church. The risen Jesus acts to save where his "name" is invoked in faith. When the apostles call on his name salvation is offered. It becomes visible in cures and exorcisms and the gift of faith itself (3:6,16). He is present in the recital of his life, death and resurrection (10:34-43; 13:16-41). Luke shows how Jesus is present in the lives of his witnesses by stamping the figure of Jesus so heavily on the apostles Peter and Paul when he parallels their powerful deeds with those of Jesus. The role of Jesus is re-enacted, too, in the sufferings in which Paul's mission involves him (9:15-16) and in his journey to and trial in Jerusalem. In the martyrdom of Stephen it is the Passion of Christ which is re-enacted.

Finally the risen Jesus is present in his disciples in the gift of the Holy Spirit who continues in them the mission which he motivated and energised in Jesus himself. Acts has rightly been called "the book of the Holy Spirit." The coming of the Spirit on the Church at Pentecost dominates the story. Just as the Father anointed Jesus with the Spirit at his baptism for his prophetic ministry in Israel (10:38), so the risen Jesus communicates the Spirit to his disciples for their prophetic ministry to the ends of the earth (2:33). It is the Spirit who makes the apostles "witnesses" of the risen Jesus, who empowers the Church to proclaim the Gospel, who is the connecting link between the time of Jesus and the time of the church.

This divine power Luke relates both to the Father and to Jesus. On the one hand the risen Jesus baptizes with the Spirit (1:5; 11:16) and the Spirit is "the Spirit of Jesus" (16:6,7); on the other the Spirit is the promise of the Father (1:4) and is poured out by Him (2:17-18). Though he states this relationship, Luke is content to leave it unclarified. He ascribes many activities to the Spirit (cf. 2:4; 5:32; 8:39; 16:7), but at times the Spirit seems to be the power of God, extension of His personality as presented in the Old Testament, at other times inseparable from the activity of the risen Jesus (cf. 10:14,19).

Whereas Paul and John consider the Holy Spirit as a force for inner individual renewal, Luke focuses on the Spirit as the source of faith and its external manifestations.

He does not ascribe to the Holy Spirit the forgiveness of sins or see his coming as the effect of baptism. For Luke the Holy Spirit comes to endow the Church for the presentation of the Gospel in convincing preaching and powerful and extraordinary deeds and to draw each aspect of its life into the task of the mission.

At Pentecost the Holy Spirit brings to birth the people of God of the New Covenant. John the Baptist had warned that the status of Israel as "children of Abraham" was no assurance of membership in this community (Lk 3:8).

From the beginning Luke has portrayed Jesus as a wedge driven into Israel, dividing it by its response to his mission (Lk 2:34-35). In particular he has distinguished "the people of God" from its leaders. The crucifixion marks the culmination of this process (Lk 23:35). It is to the death of Jesus that Luke attributes God's acquisition of His people (Acts 20:28).

By the power of the Holy Spirit the apostles become prophets of the New Covenant. Their words invite men to repentance, to a change of attitude to the crucified Christ by acknowledging him, now risen, as "Lord and Christ." Those who accept their message listen to the prophet promised by Moses whom God "raised up," separate themselves from "this perverse generation" and are saved (Acts 2:40). Those who refuse to listen are "exterminated from God's people" (Acts 3:23).

Acts is the story of God's action as he raises up children to Abraham even from the stones. The real people of God is gradually revealed in the response of Jews, Samaritans and pagans to the apostolic message. James declares in Jerusalem the wonder of God's plan in constituting for himself a people by joining pagans and Jews in a community whose hearts are purified by faith (Acts 15:14).

8) Plan

How did Luke arrange the different kinds of materials available in his sources? The basic parallelism between chapters 1-12 and 13-28 might suggest a simple division into two parts. It has often been noticed that these sections are connected by a loose parallelism of content and sequence of events which parallel, for example, the activities of Peter in the first part and Paul in the second. This parallel is noticeable particularly in the miracles they work but also in other details of their missionary activity. The parallels extend to similarities in the language in which the events are narrated. This structural parallelism can be shown to be due not to the sources he used but to Luke's own editorial activity. Thematically, however, the second volume is dominated by the command of the risen Lord at its start, "You shall be my witnesses in Jerusalem and in all Judaea and Samaria and to the ends of the earth" (1:8).

Within these main sections, namely Jerusalem, Judaea and Samaria, the ends of the earth, there are other indications of turning points in the action. There are other geographical shifts such as Paul's final journey from Jerusalem to Rome. There are also the "summaries" composed by Luke that punctuate his narrative. The best known or "major" summaries occur in the section on the early life of the community in Jerusalem (2:42-47; 4:32-35; 5:11-16), but other "minor" (e.g. 6:7; 9:31) or "numerical" (e.g. 11:21,24) summaries serve to emphasize the continuing growth of the community under God's protection.

The story can be divided as follows:

Introduction: The Change of Eras	1:1-11
Part 1 Jerusalem	1:12 - 5:42
Part 2 Judaea and Samaria	6:1 - 12:25
Part 3 To the End of the Earth	13:1 - 28:31
Section 1 - Missions of Paul and Barnabas	13:1 - 15:35
Section 2 - Missions of Paul	15:36 - 21:14
Section 3 - From Jerusalem to Rome	21:15 - 28:31

INTRODUCTION:
THE CHANGE OF ERAS.
1:1-11.

1 In the first book, O Theophilus, I have dealt with all that Jesus began to do and teach, [2]until the day when

> he was taken up, after he had given commandment through the Holy Spirit to the apostles whom he had chosen. [3]To them he presented himself alive after his passion by many proofs, appearing to them during forty days, and speaking of the kingdom of God. [4]And while staying with them he charged them not to depart from Jerusalem, but to wait for the promise of the Father, which, he said, "you heard from me, [5]for John baptized with water, but before many days you shall be baptized with the Holy Spirit.
>
> [6]So when they had come together, they asked him, "Lord, will you at this time restore the kingdom to Israel?" [7]He said to them, "It is not for you to know times or seasons which the Father has fixed by his own authority. [8]But you shall receive power when the Holy Spirit has come upon you; and you shall be my witness in Jerusalem and in all Judea and Samaria and to the end of the earth." [9]And when he had said this, as they were looking on, he was lifted up, and a cloud took him out of their sight. [10]And while they were gazing into heaven as he went, behold, two men stood by them in white robes, [11]and said "Men of Galilee, why do you stand looking into heaven? This Jesus, who was taken up from you into heaven, will come in the same way as you saw him go into heaven."

Luke follows the custom of authors of his time by commencing his second volume with an introduction recapitulating the matter of the first and outlining the subject he is to pursue. The "acts" of the apostles commence in v.12, but not before the second volume has been set in its proper context. This introduction consists of the briefest of recapitulations of Luke's Gospel (vv.1-2), a summary of the converse of Jesus with the apostles between his Resurrection and Ascension (vv.3-8), and the tableau of the Ascension (vv.9-11).

The recapitulation of volume one focusses on Jesus, the Spirit, and the apostles. From the beginning of the central section of the Gospel, Luke has pointed ahead to the "taking up" of Jesus to be accomplished in Jerusalem (Lk 9:51). Jesus "makes his way" or "goes up" to Jerusalem, there to be "taken up" into heaven. The latter term suggests that Jesus is like the prophet Elijah (cf. 2 Kgs 2:9-12, Sir 48:9), a comparison of which Luke is fond. Apart from referring to the miracles and teaching of Jesus what is recalled is his choice of the apostles and final command to them. For Luke, the "apostles" are "the Twelve," the inner circle chosen from the larger group of disciples who followed him to Jerusalem. Jesus chose them after prayer (Lk 6:12-16) and appointed them as leaders over the twelve tribes of Israel (Lk 22:30), a chosen people whose true identity will be gradually revealed in the course of Acts until it is finally declared by James at the Council of Jerusalem (Acts 15:14). Though the R.S.V. connects the phrase "through the Holy Spirit" to Jesus' command to the apostles, it should rather be referred to his choice of the Twelve. The men who were to be the link between Jesus and the Church were chosen under the direction of the Spirit.

After this recapitulation of the first volume, literary custom called for a statement of the matter of the second. The following verses (vv.3-8), however, are concerned with the dealings of the risen Jesus and the apostles in the forty day interim between the Resurrection and Ascension. Luke doubles back, taking up and enlarging on elements of the final chapter of the Gospel in such a way that the mission and life of the Church depicted in Acts will be seen to arise from the association of the apostles with the risen Jesus. Thus it is Jesus who "shows himself alive" (cf. Lk 24:23), "appears" (Lk 24:33-34), "offers proofs" (Lk 24:36-43). The faith of the apostles in the risen Jesus is itself the work of the risen Jesus. He "eats with" (v.4, rather than R.S.V. "staying with") them, which may suggest the origin of the "breaking of bread" (Acts 2:42) as a continuation of the fellowship of the apostles with the risen Lord. He "speaks to them about the Kingdom of God," thus originating the proclamation of the Kingdom to be described in Acts (e.g. 8:12; 19:8; 20:25). Paul at its conclusion (28:31) will be preaching in Rome the Kingdom revealed to the apostles in Jerusalem at its beginning. "Forty days" is a symbolic figure. It probably parallels the period prior to the public preaching of the apostles with the forty days prior to the beginning of Jesus' ministry (Lk 4:2). It may also suggest that the apostles imbibed the teaching of the risen Jesus thoroughly since it was the period stipulated as necessary for a disciple to master the teaching of a rabbi.

The command referred to in v.2 is spelled out in v.4 (cf. Lk 24:49). It is prohibition and promise. They must not leave Jerusalem but await there "what the Father had promised," the promise of the gift of the Spirit they had heard from Jesus. Luke ascribes (v.5) a saying to the risen Jesus very similar to one he has ascribed to John the Baptist (Lk 3:16). What will happen to the apostles will be a "baptism," but by contrast with the water-baptism of John they are soon to be baptised with the Holy Spirit.

Luke was perfectly well aware of stories of appearances of the risen Lord in Galilee. That he confines the appearances in his story to Jerusalem and its surroundings is due to his systematic presentation. For him Jerusalem is central. He conceives the story of salvation as a "going-up" of Jesus to Jerusalem, a "taking up" of Jesus from Jerusalem into heaven, a "descent of the Holy Spirit" on the apostles in Jerusalem, and a movement of the mission out from its centre in Jerusalem to "the ends of the earth."

The question of the apostles and the answer of the risen Jesus (vv.6-8) provide an answer to questions that had been asked many times before Luke wrote (cf. 1 Thess 5:1). The coming of the Spirit is not the immediate prelude to the restoration of Israel promised by the prophets (cf. Acts 3:19) but so often debased, in popular expectations, to nationalistic triumphalism; nor is it a basis for the kind of calculation of "times and seasons" of God's final intervention dear to apocalyptic literature. Rather it is the endowment of the apostles with power for their function as "witnesses." Just as the conception of Jesus, "Son of the Most High," was due to the coming of the Holy Spirit on the Virgin Mary (Lk 1:35), so the inception of the mission of the Church is brought about by a coming of the Holy Spirit on the apostles. "Witness" is perhaps the earliest term to designate the primary and essential function of the Twelve (cf. Acts 1:22; 2:32; 3:15) and the central object of their testimony is the Resurrection (e.g. Acts 1:21; 4:33). The mission command of the risen Jesus is more detailed in the four-stage development of v.8 than in the two-stage statement in Luke's Gospel (Lk 24:47-49). Here Luke is offering the programme his story is to follow: Jerusalem (Acts 1-7), Judea and Samaria (Acts 8-12), "to the ends of the earth" (Acts 13-28). The phrase "to the ends of the earth" harks back to Is 49:6, the prophecy of universal salvation to be achieved through the work of the Servant of God (cf. Acts 2:32; 13:47). Luke's story of the spread of the Gospel to Rome which exemplifies "the ends of the earth" will illustrate the fulfilment of God's plan of universal salvation already announced by the prophet.

After the promise that the Holy Spirit will come, the introduction concludes with the departure of Jesus (vv.9-11). Luke was aware that others made no distinction between the Resurrection and the Ascension - at times he writes this way himself (Lk 24:26; Acts 2:32-33; 5:30-31). In fact he is the only New Testament writer to present them as separate events in chronological sequence, but even this he does in different ways. In his first volume the Ascension is placed at the close of one Easter day of appearances. It comes as a solemn finale, the accomplishment of the Paschal mystery summarized in a solemn blessing at Bethany which initiates the joyful worship of the Church. In Acts the Ascension comes at the end of forty days and serves as a prelude to the continuing mission of the Church in the world until Jesus' return in glory. Luke constructs the scene by using conventional biblical images to explain the meaning of the era of the Church. The description of the Ascension is very brief; the accent falls on the responses of the apostles.

As he is giving his mission charge, while the "witnesses" look on, Jesus is "taken up." A cloud, sign and veil of God's presence (Ex 24:15-18; Lk 9:34-35) puts an end to his visible presence. Jesus enters into God's own realm. "Two men in white robes," divine messengers (Lk 9:30; 24:4), explain on God's behalf the meaning of the event to the watching apostles. The "journey" of Jesus to God is completed. But "he shall come," and in the same glorious manner. The insistence of the story on the "seeing" (vv.9,10,11) of the apostles as Jesus is "taken up" may suggest a final detail in Luke's comparison of Jesus with Elijah; since his disciples see him as he is taken up, they are assured, like Elisha, that they will receive his spirit to continue his mission (2 Kgs 2:10,12).

The Ascension marks the close of an era. Jesus' journey to God has been completed by his "taking up" into heaven. It likewise signals the beginning of a new era, that of the mission of the Church which is about to be inaugurated. Just as God's unpredictable, invincible power, the Holy Spirit, made of the life of Jesus the gift of God's salvation to his countrymen in their time and place, so that same power will come on his witnesses to proclaim that salvation to others, first of all in Jerusalem and then "to the ends of the earth" for God's work is incomplete until His offer has been proclaimed to all. The mission of the Church is the command of the Risen Lord.

These things, luminously clear to Luke from the lessons of the last half-century, were not nearly so clear to those who participated in them. With the benefit of hindsight Luke presents the story of the mission to his reader in advance as the gradual unfolding of the implications of Jesus' return to God, under the guidance of the Holy Spirit, through human responses to the events he is to narrate.

Part I

Witnesses in Jerusalem

1:12 — 5:42

PART I
WITNESSES IN JERUSALEM

THE RESTORATION OF THE TWELVE. 1:12-26.

[12]Then they returned to Jerusalem from the mount called Olivet, which is near Jerusalem, a sabbath day's journey away; [13]and when they had entered, they went up to the upper room, where they were staying, Peter and John and James and Andrew, Philip and Thomas, Bartholomew and Matthew, James the son of Alphaeus and Simon the Zealot and Judas the son of James. [14]All these with one accord devoted themselves to prayer, together with the women and Mary the mother of Jesus, and with his brothers.

[15]In those days Peter stood up among the brethren (the company of persons was in all about a hundred and twenty), and said, [16]"Brethren, the scripture had to be fulfilled, which the Holy Spirit spoke beforehand by the mouth of David, concerning Judas who was guide to those who arrested Jesus. [17]For he was numbered among us, and was allotted his share in this ministry. [18](Now this man bought a field with the reward of his wickedness; and falling headlong he burst open in the middle and all his bowels gushed out. [19]And it became known to all the inhabitants of Jerusalem, so that the field was called in their language Akeldama, that is, Field of Blood.) [20]For it is written in the book of Psalms,

'Let his habitation become desolate,

and let there be no one to live in it'; and
'His office let another take.'

[21]So one of the men who have accompanied us during all the time that the Lord Jesus went in and out among us, [22]beginning from the baptism of John until the day when he was taken up from us—one of these men must become with us a witness to his resurrection." [23]And they put forward two, Joseph called Barsabbas, who was surnamed Justus, and Matthias. [24]And they prayed and said, "Lord, who knowest the hearts of all men, show which one of these two thou hast chosen [25]to take the place in this ministry and apostleship from which Judas turned aside, to go to his own place." [26]And they cast lots for them, and the lot fell on Matthias; and he was enrolled with the eleven apostles.

Luke separates the promise of the Spirit from its fulfilment at Pentecost by the story of the choice of a successor for Judas. The interruption seems to delay the action, but it is deliberately done and essential in his understanding of the position of "The Twelve" in the Church that is to be born.

His first volume has shown that when Jesus "chose twelve whom he named apostles" (Lk 6:13) he took a decisive step in preparing the leaders of the people of God who would replace the Jewish leaders who rejected him. He sent them out to preach with his authority (Lk 9:1-6), associated them with himself in his ministry (Lk 9:10-11), and finally, at the Last Supper, conferred on them his own authority as leaders of Israel (Lk 22:30). "The Twelve" were the divinely appointed leaders of the new Israel which gathered around them and under their authority. As a group they constituted the nucleus of the people whose unity they symbolised and embodied, as Israel's twelve tribes were embodied in their twelve patriarchs. The apostasy of Judas, then, was much more serious than the infidelity, however horrible, of an individual disciple. When "one of the number of the Twelve" (Lk 22:3), a man "numbered among us and allotted his share of this ministry" (Acts 1:16-17) became "guide of those who captured Jesus" the integrity of the group as nucleus was shattered. Established by the choice of Jesus, that integrity is restored by his choice before the coming of the Holy Spirit.

Luke underlines the centrality of the apostles in the nascent Church (vv.12-14). Peter's speech illumines the scandal of Judas' defection by the light of the Scriptures and explains the function of the apostles (vv.15-22), and the election of Matthias reconstitutes the circle of the Twelve (vv.23-26).

The apostles return to Jerusalem. This "return to Jerusalem" is almost a refrain of Luke's (cf. Lk 24:9,33,52; Acts 8:25; 13:13; 22:17). The eleven are listed for a second time; a comparison of Luke's two lists (Lk 6:13-16; Acts 1:13) shows that John has been promoted to second in the list in view of the part he will play alongside Peter in the following chapters. Together with them are "the women, and Mary the mother of Jesus, and his brothers." The women disciples of Jesus have been mentioned in the story of the Crucifixion and again at the tomb; they have seen the crucified Jesus and his dead body in the tomb (Lk 23:49,55). "Mary the mother of Jesus" has been presented as a model of the faith of the Church during the earthly life of Jesus and remains so in the new era (Lk 1:45; 11:28). "The brothers of Jesus" are probably mentioned in view of the position that the most celebrated of them, James, is to occupy in Jerusalem (Acts 12:17; 15:13). A Lucan summary (v.14) depicts apostles and disciples as being "of one mind," a characteristic phrase of Luke's to express the unity and harmony of the primitive community (cf. Acts 2:46; 4:24), and "sedulous in prayer," the attitude of Jesus (cf. Lk 3:21; 6:12 etc.) that will be continued in the Church in which prayer is the preparation for any decisive event (Acts 4:24-30; 13:2 etc.)

Amongst the disciples and apostles Peter takes the initiative. He acts for the first time as confirmer of the faith of his brethren (Lk 22:32). This is the first of eight discourses attributed to Peter in Acts, five of them in its first five chapters. It shows the new manner of understanding the Scriptures opened up to the apostles by their faith in the risen Jesus (Lk 24:45) and falls into two parts, the first concerning the defection of Judas (vv.15-20), the second his replacement (vv.21-22), each of them explained as falling within a divine pattern attested in the Scriptures which "must" be fulfilled (vv.16,21). The same divine necessity that governed the life, death and resurrection of Jesus (cf. Lk 4:43; 22:37; 24:44 etc.) embraces within its scope the defection of Judas and calls for his replacement.

In explaining the defection of Judas as a "fulfilment" of the Scriptures Luke is far from offering a psychological explanation of his treachery. Matthew, too, tells the story of the death of Judas (Mt 27:3-10). Both he and Luke draw on stories in circulation before them concerned with the field known in Jerusalem as Hakeldama and both are concerned to place the events in the context of the Scriptures which show the fate of Judas as the typical death of a traitor. Matthew harks back to the story of David to recall that the first king of the Davidic line suffered from the treachery of Achitophel, trusted friend and counsellor (2 Sam 17:23) whose fate Judas finally underwent. Luke shows Judas as one of those who abandon the Lord and persecute the righteous man (Wis 3:10; 4:19). Whereas for Matthew it is the blood of Jesus which gave its name to Hakeldama, for Luke the gory manner of Judas' death on the farm he bought with the price of his betrayal explains the title "Field of Blood." The desolation of that property, symbolic of Judas' fate, was prophesied in advance in Psalm 69, widely regarded in the early Church as a prophecy of the death of Christ.

Peter finds the necessity of a replacement predicted in Psalm 109. Judas' share in the ministry of the Twelve is to be taken by another. Verses 21-22 are an important statement of Luke's idea of what "apostles" are. They are qualified by sharing in the life of Jesus from the beginning of the public ministry in the baptism of John up till the Ascension as "witnesses of the Resurrection." Through their corporate sharing in the events of the career of Jesus the apostles connect later generations with their beginnings. There is a special quality to this "witness" to the Risen Jesus in that they testify to the identity of the Risen Jesus with the Jesus they accompanied from Galilee.

This was not the only view in the early Church as to what constituted an "apostle." Paul's was different (cf. Gal 1:1; 1 Cor 15:2-9) and Luke's would seem to exclude Paul from the title, though he will later bestow it on Paul and Barnabas (14:4,14) to underline their continuity with the Twelve.

The choice of the Twelve was an act of Jesus during his earthly life; the choice of the man by whom it will be reconstituted is equally a choice of Jesus. The community addresses Jesus in prayer to make his present choice known. This is manifested in the casting of lots. With the choice of Matthias the integrity of the apostolic college is restored by its Lord and the Twelve are reconstituted as nucleus of the people to be born at Pentecost.

Luke is not rehearsing clearly remembered and accurately recorded happenings in chronological sequence. The sequel of events after the death of Jesus was not as simple as a series of appearances terminated at the end of forty days. It is not known when Judas died; the community these verses depict is already somewhat organised. In particular, the discourse of Peter is a composition of Luke and the position it occupies reflects Luke's theology more than a systematic chronology. It is really addressed to the reader, as can be seen in the parenthesis of v.19 ("the field was called, in their language"—the language Peter is supposedly speaking) and in the use of the Greek translation of the Old Testament in v.20 (Ps 69:25 in the Hebrew text refers to a camp and tents, the Greek translation to a farm or homestead and the argument depends on this item). Luke draws on stories current in Jerusalem about the field called Hakeldama and his use of the Scriptures reflects that of Christians before him; the language and the conception of the role of the apostles is characteristically his.

PENTECOST. "THEY WERE ALL FILLED WITH THE HOLY SPIRIT." 2:1-11.

2 When the day of Pentecost had come, they were all together in one place. [2]And suddenly a sound came from heaven like the rush of a mighty wind, and it filled all the house where they were sitting. [3]And there appeared to them tongues as of fire, distributed and resting on each one of them. [4]And they were all filled with the Holy Spirit and began to speak in other tongues, as the Spirit gave them utterance.

[5]Now there were dwelling in Jerusalem Jews, devout men from every nation under heaven. [6]And at this sound the multitude came together, and they were bewildered, because each one heard them speaking in his own language. [7]And they were amazed and wondered, saying, "Are not all these who are speaking Galileans? [8]And how is it that we hear, each of us in his own native language? [9]Parthians and Medes and Elamites and residents of Mesopotamia, Judea and Cappadocia, Pontus and Asia, [10]Phrygia and Pamphylia, Egypt and the parts of Libya belonging to Cyrene, and visitors from Rome, both Jews and proselytes, [11]Cretans and Arabians, we hear them telling in our own tongues the mighty works of God."

Luke has left us with a tableau of the Jerusalem community, its nucleus re-established, awaiting in eager and prayerful expectation for the fulfilment of the promise of a "baptism with the Holy Spirit." The era of the Church will commence with a coming of the Holy Spirit on the community parallel with the coming of the Spirit on Jesus at the commencement of his ministry. The Pentecost story is a tableau of the community born as the People of Yahweh of the new covenant by the power of the Holy Spirit, and already launched from its inception in Jerusalem on its mission to people of all nations by its initial Spirit-powered proclamation of "the mighty works of God." The tableau is followed by a speech of Peter which offers a prophetic explanation of the events (vv.12-41) which, as so often in the ministry of Jesus, have divided the onlookers.

Luke was not the first to tell the story. At times it can be seen that he is inserting elements into a previous account. Repetitions (e.g. vv.8,11) are like pieces left over or connecting links where an insertion has forced repetition of details. The speech of Peter is a three-minute summary, important principally for the part it plays in the overall direction of Luke's book. These were the kind of things the first preachers used to say, but time has shown the significance of the beginnings in their historical sequel and a long community reflection on the Scriptures has discovered in prophets and psalms the earlier hints of what God intended. The world-wide Church which Theophilus knows began in an initial explosion of faith in the risen Jesus and with the proclamation of what God had done through him.

The event is depicted in symbolic language (vv.1-4). "Pentecost" simply means "fiftieth," the feast celebrated seven weeks after the gathering of the first sheaf (Lev 23:15-16). Originally a harvest festival it was later organised into one of the three great Jewish feasts that brought throngs of pilgrims to the Temple. In the time of Jesus many Jews regarded it as a celebration of the giving of the Law to Moses on Mount Sinai, the inauguration of the covenant that made of Israel the People of Yahweh. The Essenes at Qumran regarded it as a memorial and renewal of the covenant.

Luke's tableau recalls details of the biblical story of the giving of the Law but also of elements of rabbinical commentaries on the story told in Exodus in which Israel's teachers tried to show the universal importance of the giving of the Law. Elaborating on Ex 20:18 "now when all the people saw the thunderings and the lightnings and the sound of the trumpet and the mountain smoking," it had been said that the voice of God divided into seventy tongues, so that every nation heard the Law in its own language. What Luke points to is the birth of the People of Yahweh of the new covenant, the fulfilment of which is proclaimed to people of all nations so that "the day of Pentecost was fulfilled."

"All together in one," like the Israelites on Sinai (cf. Ex 19:1,8), in a union of hearts as well as of place, there comes a loud noise (cf. Ex 19:16; 20:18). It comes "from heaven," as had the Spirit on Jesus at his Baptism (Lk 3:22). The noise is like that of a violent gust of wind, the breath issued from Yahweh's nostrils (Ex 15:8,10), a messenger carrying His word to the extremities of the earth to execute His will. This "filled all the house" as the Spirit will fill all those who dwell in it.

Visual images succeed those of sound. In the customary biblical terms to denote a divine communication or a manifestation of something of the divine reality, "there appeared" something like "fire" (cf. Ex 19:18; 24:17), symbolic of God's fiery judgment inaugurating the end of times, His purifying power promised by John (Lk 3:16) and Jesus (Acts 1:5). The basic image is that of "tongues" and it is here that the final emphasis falls, for the proclamation of the apostles is the instrument by which God's purification of His People will be achieved. Isaiah's lips were purified by a fiery coal from the heavenly sanctuary to proclaim God's message (Is 6:7); it is to be the Holy Spirit, the power of God, which consecrates their message and is conveyed by it.

The story emphasises the symbolism of "tongues." They "began to speak in other tongues, as the Spirit gave them utterance." Devout Jews from "every nation under heaven" hear their speech "each in his own tongue." Luke inserts a list of nations (vv.9-11) into the story to underline the universal import of the happening. It is likely that the detail of the "division of tongues" refers to the story of Babel

(Gen 11:6-9; cf. Deut 32:8). The nations divided since Babel are re-united by the apostolic proclamation. The scene also points to the future Luke is to describe. The tempestuous wind of the Spirit will scatter them to the ends of the earth and the Gospel will be proclaimed to all men in their own tongue.

Analysed in its own terms Luke's picture depicts the birth of the Church and its future mission. Individual details of the tableau cause difficulties when taken separately. The reason for the mockery that follows (v.13) and the similar phenomena regarded as parallel to these in the coming of the Spirit on the pagans in the house of Cornelius (Acts 10:46) suggest the kind of ecstatic "speaking in tongues" familiar to Paul in Corinth (1 Cor 13-14). But other verses refer to intelligible speech in foreign languages (vv.6,8,11,12) and it is in this that the story is symbolic of the Church's proclamation. Reducing Luke's tableau to a photograph, that is, to the observable details of the occasion, is difficult because his sources are unknown and it is unsure how much of his picture is due to his later developed insight.

Luke will tell the story of other "comings of the Holy Spirit" such as those that preceded the baptism of the pagans by Peter (Acts 10:44) and followed the baptism of Paul's converts in Ephesus (Acts 19:6). His second volume can be regarded as a series of "Pentecosts," each of them marking a further step in the advance of the mission and further clarifying the divine intention latent in the first. It seems that details of the latter provide some of Luke's colours in painting the picture of the first.

PETER'S SPEECH.
"GOD HAS MADE HIM LORD AND CHRIST."
2:12-40.

[12]And all were amazed and perplexed, saying to one another, "What does this mean?" [13]But others mocking said, "They are filled with new wine."

[14]But Peter, standing with the eleven, lifted up his voice and addressed them, "Men of Judea and all who dwell in Jerusalem, let this be known to you, and give ear to my words. [15]For these men are not drunk, as you suppose, since it is only the third hour of the day; [16]but this is what was spoken by the prophet Joel:

[17]'And in the last days it shall be, God declares,
that I will pour out my Spirit upon all flesh,
and your sons and your daughters shall prophesy,
and your young men shall see visions,
and your old men shall dream dreams;
[18]yea, and on my menservants and my maidservants in those days
I will pour out my Spirit; and they shall prophesy.
[19]And I will show wonders in the heaven above
and signs on the earth beneath,
blood, and fire, and vapour of smoke;
[20]the sun shall be turned into darkness and the moon into blood,
before the day of the Lord comes,
the great and manifest day.
[21]And it shall be that whoever calls on the name of the Lord shall be saved.'

[22]"Men of Israel, hear these words: Jesus of Nazareth, a man attested to you by God with mighty works and wonders and signs which God did through him in your midst, as you yourselves know—[23]this Jesus, delivered up according to the definite plan and foreknowledge of God, you crucified and killed by the hands of lawless men. [24]But God raised him up, having loosed the pangs of death, because it was not possible for him to be held by it. [25]For David says concerning him,

'I saw the Lord always before me, for he is at my right hand that I may not be shaken;
[26]therefore my heart was glad, and my tongue rejoiced;
moreover my flesh will dwell in hope.
[27]For thou wilt not abandon my soul to Hades,
nor let thy Holy One see corruption.

[28]Thou hast made known to me the ways of life;
thou wilt make me full of gladness with thy presence.'

[29]"Brethren, I may say to you confidently of the patriarch David that he both died and was buried, and his tomb is with us to this day. [30]Being therefore a prophet, and knowing that God had sworn with an oath to him that he would set one of his descendants upon his throne, [31]he foresaw and spoke of the resurrection of the Christ, that he was not abandoned to Hades, nor did his flesh see corruption. [32]This Jesus God raised up, and of that we all are witnesses. [33]Being therefore exalted at the right hand of God, and having received from the Father the promise of the Holy Spirit, he has poured out this which you see and hear. [34]For David did not ascend into the heavens; but he himself says,

'The Lord said to my Lord, Sit at my right hand,
[35]till I make thy enemies a stool for thy feet.'

[36]Let all the house of Israel therefore know assuredly that God has made him both Lord and Christ, this Jesus whom you crucified."

[37]Now when they heard this they were cut to the heart, and said to Peter and the rest of the apostles, "Brethren, what shall we do?" [38]And Peter said to them, "Repent, and be baptized every one of you in the name of Jesus Christ for the forgiveness of your sins; and you shall receive the gift of the Holy Spirit. [39]For the promise is to you and to your children and to all that are far off, every one whom the Lord our God calls to him." [40]And he testified with many other words and exhorted them, saying, "Save yourselves from this crooked generation."

When God acts men are brought to wonder and perplexity; they are divided by their responses. His acts call for explanations. It is the function of the prophet to explain the events through his insight into God's plan. The discourse of Peter which follows the story of Pentecost is a prophetic explanation of the event in the light of the Scriptures which culminates in a proclamation of Christ as Lord. The first prophet of the era of the Spirit explains and proclaims its inauguration. Just as Jesus after his anointing as a prophet by the Spirit in his baptism (Acts 10:38) inaugurated his ministry in a programmatic discourse concerning the coming of the Spirit in the synagogue at Nazareth (Lk 4:16-21), so now Peter inaugurates the ministry of the Church by a sermon proclaiming the coming of the Spirit on the Church.

This is not the first utterance of Peter. He has already spoken in a discourse to the community leading to the reconstitution of the Twelve. The Pentecost discourse differs from it in that it is a direct presentation of the Christian message to others, to Jews. Through Peter's address Luke offers to his own readers a first sample of the preaching of the apostles, for Peter does not stand alone. He stands "with the eleven"; it is the witness of the group that he utters. Peter's regular use of "we" in these early chapters is no royal plural from a Galilean fisherman suddenly conscious of the position to which he has been promoted but Luke's deliberate association of Peter with the apostolic college (cf. 3:12,15; 4:9; 5:32). This discourse has been called "the most finished and polished specimen of the apostolic preaching, placed as it were in the shop window of the Jerusalem Church and of Luke's narrative."

An analysis of the major missionary and apologetic discourses of Acts shows a number of common underlying elements arranged in a similar pattern. An introduction connects the discourse with the thread of the narrative. This is followed by a summary of the earthly ministry, death and resurrection of Jesus, followed by Scriptural proof of his Messiahship and an offer of remission of sins to those who accept the message. Sometimes a reference to the Parousia is included. These sermons are not only or even primarily accounts of how the Christian message was proclaimed in the past; they are Luke's own presentation of the Good News to his readers.

The Pentecost discourse can be divided into three parts, each opening with solemn words of address to the audience and closing with a Scriptural quotation. The first (vv.14-21) adduces the prophecy of Joel as explanation of the Pentecost phenomena, the second(vv.22-28) recites the life, death and resurrection of Jesus and concludes with a citation of Psalm 16, the third (vv.29-35) argues from Psalms 16 and 110 that the Messiahship of Jesus is proven by his resurrection. The proclamation of the Lordship of Jesus is followed by a dialogue between preacher and audience (vv.37-40), calling for repentance in view of the remission of sins.

It is a widespread belief in Israel that the heavens had been closed and the Holy Spirit had descended on no one, prophet or leader, since the last of the canonical prophets, Haggai, Zechariah and Malachi. Peter claims that in what has happened God has lived up to the promise He made through Joel (Joel 2:28-32). The prophecy envisaged an outpouring of God's spirit on "all mankind." The phenomena that had accompanied the activity of the prophets would be repeated on a grandiose scale. In the conventional images of prophetic and apocalyptic writings it describes the cosmic disturbances that are to precede the "Day of the Lord" and promises salvation to faithful Israelites, those who call on the name of the Lord," that is, Yahweh.

We get a clearer view of what the prophetic texts meant for Luke in noticing the additions or changes he has made to the text so as to indicate its significance in his story. He adds "in the last days, God says" (v.17) to make it clear that the coming of the Spirit at Pentecost is a definitive act of God, something unrepeatable which commences the eschatological era. He adds "and they shall prophesy" (v.17) to show that the powerful action of the Holy Spirit in the Church will be manifested especially in the gift of prophecy and exemplified in the very discourse he is offering. Joel spoke of "portents in the heavens and on the earth blood and fire and columns of smoke"; Luke distinguishes between "wonders in the heaven above" and "signs on the earth beneath." The Ascension is a "wonder in the heaven above" though only a preview of the final wonder in the return of Jesus in glory; the presence of the Spirit in the Church will guarantee that "signs and wonders" comparable to those of Moses (e.g. Ex 4:8,9,17) and those which accredited Jesus as a prophet (Acts 2:22) will continue, in order to bring men to "call on the name of the Lord" in order that they may be saved. The conclusion of the speech will show that in this respect, too, Peter's speech is a model of this Spirit-guided prophetic activity leading men to call on the name of Jesus for it is he who is, now, "both Lord and Christ." Already this programmatic discourse throws light on what Luke's second volume is intended to show and underlies all the rest of the references to the Spirit and to "signs and wonders" in the rest of this book.

The second section (vv.22-28) commences the detailed interpretation of the Pentecost event as the culmination of the career of Jesus. His earthly life is presented in very simple terms (v.22) as that of a prophet like Moses authenticated by God. Luke says not a word about the saving significance of the death of Jesus (v.23); he accuses the men of Jerusalem for their responsibility in it and simply states that even the death of Jesus was "according to the definite plan and foreknowledge of God." The wickedness of the Jews resulting in his ignominious death heightens the wonder of God's act in raising him (v.24). That all this, death as well as resurrection, fell within the scope of God's plan Peter proceeds to prove on the basis of the Scriptures.

The third section (vv.29-35) draws out the significance of the resurrection by establishing it as the fulfilment of two prophetic promises (Pss 16:8-11; 10:1). The first is not fulfilled in the history of David; David is dead and buried, his tomb is a local monument. The words were spoken by David in prophecy of "the Christ," of the resurrection of the Davidic Messiah to come. It is possible that Jesus is compared also with Moses (v.33), for Jewish commentators read Psalm 68 as an image of Moses ascending Mount Sinai to receive the Law as God's gift to His People. Jesus exalted into heaven brings God's gift of the Spirit. Peter invokes the promise of Psalm 110 as fulfilled in the "exaltation" of Jesus by which God establishes him as the "Christ" and the "Lord" of whom the two promises spoke.

The climax of the discourse is reached in the call for all Israel to acknowledge Jesus of Nazareth, crucified and now "risen" or "exalted" as the one whom God has established as "Lord and Christ," exercising his newly acquired function by pouring out on God's People the Spirit he has received from God. Kyrios or "Lord" is a name reserved to Yahweh Himself in the Old Testament; the bestowal of this name on Jesus in his exaltation signifies that by God's gift Jesus exercises powers that previously had been reserved to Yahweh alone, the divine power to communicate salvation and to judge.

A question from the audience (v.37) shows the power of Peter's prophetic words for conversion. It typifies the proper response (cf. Lk 3:11) and this occasions a call for repentance (v.38). Repentance (metanoia) is a change of heart, a "total capsizing of the life of a man who henceforth follows the path that leads to God." For the inhabitants of Jerusalem it means a total reversal of their attitude to the Jesus whom they crucified and whom they must acknowledge as "Lord and Christ," a sharing in the life and attitudes of the community into which they were initiated by "baptism in the name of Jesus Christ." This brings forgiveness of sins and the gift of the Spirit, the great realities of salvation. The gift is given to the children of the promise, those who separate themselves from "this evil generation" to form the new Israel, to constitute a people made up of Jews but also, in the phrase of Isaiah 57:19, "all that are far off." From its first proclamation the apostolic preaching points ahead to the extension of God's promise to the Gentiles.

SUMMARY: THE COMMUNITY CREATED BY THE SPIRIT. 2:41-47.

[41]So those who received his word were baptized, and there were added that day about three thousand souls.

> [42]And they devoted themselves to the apostles' teaching and fellowship, to the breaking of bread and the prayers.
> [43]And fear came upon every soul; and many wonders and signs were done through the apostles. [44]And all who believed were together and had all things in common; [45]and they sold their possessions and goods and distributed them to all, as any had need. [46]And day by day, attending the temple together and breaking bread in their homes, they partook of food with glad and generous hearts, [47]praising God and having favour with all the people. And the Lord added to their number day by day those who were being saved.

Much of the Acts is punctuated by what could be called "growth notes," short sentences underlining the numerical growth of the community or the spread of the Good News (e.g. 2:41; 6:7; 9:31; 12:24). The extended picture of the Jerusalem community is characterised by three larger "summaries" (2:42-47; 4:32-35; 5:12-16), brief tableaux bringing out essential features of its life. They serve two main purposes: the one preparatory (thus 2:43 prepares for the narrative of the cure of the lame man) and the other generalising (thus 2:44 ascribes to the whole community a community of goods which 4:34,35 shows to have been practised by people of means).

Placed as it is after the first missionary discourse and the conversions that establish the growing community, this first summary features the four central, if not constitutive, elements of the Church's life (v.42): sedulous attention to the teaching of the apostles, community of life, the breaking of bread and prayer. These four elements are elaborated (vv.43-47). "Wonders and signs" demonstrate the authority of the apostles' teaching. Though described in terms reminiscent of Hellenistic cliches concerning friendship, their sharing of possessions is not that of "friends" but "believers," expressive of the unity of faith. Like Jesus they participate in the worship of the Temple. What separates them from other Israelites in this respect is the rite of

people, "Men of Israel, why do you wonder at this, or why do you stare at us, as though by our own power or piety we had made him walk? [13]The God of Abraham and of Isaac and of Jacob, the God of our fathers, glorified his servant Jesus, whom you delivered up and denied in the presence of Pilate, when he had decided to release him. [14]But you denied the Holy and Righteous One, and asked for a murderer to be granted to you, [15]and killed the Author of life, whom God raised from the dead. To this we are witnesses. [16]And his name, by faith in his name, has made this man strong whom you see and know; and the faith which is through Jesus has given the man this perfect health in the presence of you all.

[17]"And now, brethren, I know that you acted in ignorance, as did also your rulers. [18]But what God foretold by the mouth of all the prophets, that his Christ should suffer, he thus fulfilled. [19]Repent therefore, and turn again, that your sins may be blotted out, that times of refreshing may come from the presence of the Lord, [20]and that he may send the Christ appointed for you, Jesus, [21]whom heaven must receive until the time for establishing all that God spoke by the mouth of his holy prophets from of old. [22]Moses said, 'The Lord God will raise up for you a prophet from your brethren as he raised me up. You shall listen to him in whatever he tells you. [23]And it shall be that every soul that does not listen to that prophet shall be destroyed from the people.' [24]And all the prophets who have spoken, from Samuel and those who came afterwards, also proclaimed these days. [25]You are the sons of the prophets and of the covenant which God gave to your fathers, saying to Abraham, 'And in your posterity shall all the families of the earth be blessed.' [26]God, having raised up his servant, sent him to you first, to bless you in turning every one of you from your wickedness."

Following the pattern already established, the miracle is followed by a discourse which is a prophetic interpretation of the event as a fulfilment of God's plan sketched in the

Scriptures. The cure of the lame man is a sign of God's "glorification" of His Servant. Though parallel in structure to the Pentecost discourse, it is distinctive in the severity of its indictment and the urgency and motivation of its call to conversion. The two direct addreses to the audience (vv.12,17) indicate its two sections.

Peter's starting-point is the "wonder of all the people" at the spectacle of the cured man clinging to the two apostles. To the rhetorical question "by whose power" the miracle has been worked he answers that it was worked by God through Jesus. This power to save is the way God has "glorified" him as his "Servant" in accordance with His promise (Is 52:13), a "glorification" which is a total reversal of the sinful action of the inhabitants of Jerusalem in delivering Jesus to Pilate and denying him even after the governor's decision to release him (cf. Lk 23:4,14,22). Their action is contrasted with God's. They requested "a murderer" instead of "the holy one and the righteous one" (titles practically synonymous with "the Servant"), and "the author of life you put to death." The Resurrection is thus God's establishment of Jesus as Saviour, a salvation manifested in the "perfect health" of the lame man. With verse 16 Peter has returned to his starting point. The sentence is grammatically cumbersome but it ascribes both the cure and the necessary faith on the part of the sick man to the "Name" of Jesus.

As in the Pentecost discourse the death of Jesus is explained in the most general way as indicated by the Scriptures. The ignominy of the Passion serves as a foil for the Resurrection, God's triumphant vindication. The recall of the trial and death of Jesus is used as a motive for repentance, the change of attitude that will follow their acceptance of the apostolic preaching. In the call to conversion (v.17) Peter exculpates his audience on the grounds of their previous ignorance, a plea that becomes groundless now that the apostles bear witness to the Resurrection which manifests God's attitude to Jesus. To "repentance" Luke adds the twin term "conversion" so familiar to the prophets.

For Jews, worshippers of the one true God, this implies a "turning from" a wayward life back to the demands of the covenant, to conduct which is an effective acknowledgement of Yahweh as God indeed by acceptance of the Saviour He has sent. The motivation of this conversion (vv.19-21) is unique in Luke's presentation of the apostolic preaching. The risen Jesus is depicted in terms reminiscent of the prophecy of Malachi (4:5-6), like Elijah who must return to prepare the coming of the Day of Yahweh. He has been "received into heaven" where he awaits as Messiah-designate for as long as the final period granted for the conversion of Israel lasts. The result of that conversion will be the restoration of Israel to its final condition as the true gathering of the People of Yahweh, the ideal of zealous reforming Jews since the time of the Exile. It is this hope which is referred to in the term "the times of refreshment" which, Peter asserts, their conversion will hasten.

Luke joins two texts (Deut 18:15-18; Lev 23:29) in one composite Scriptural citation (vv.22-23) to show that the Resurrection has also fulfilled the promise made by Moses that God "will raise up for you a prophet from your brethen as he raised me up." The Risen Jesus is this prophet, raised up by God and now speaking through the apostles. Refusal to hear his message incurs the terrible threat of extermination from the People of Yahweh, a fate all the more terrible for Jews, "the sons of the prophets," heirs of the covenant and the blessing to Abraham, a blessing offered to the Jews first already by Jesus in his earthly life when God sent him to "turn each one of you from your wickedness."

THE APOSTLES AND THE SANHEDRIN. "WE CANNOT BUT SPEAK . . ." 4:1-22.

4 And as they were speaking to the people, the priests and the captain of the temple and the Sadducces came upon them, [2]annoyed because they were teaching the people and proclaiming in Jesus the resurrection from the dead. [3]And they arrested them and put them in custody until the morrow, for it was already evening. [4]But many of those who heard the word believed; and the number of the men came to about five thousand.

[5]On the morrow their rulers and elders and scribes were gathered together in Jerusalem, [6]with Annas the high priest and Caiaphas and John and Alexander, and all who were of the high-priestly family. [7]And when they had set them in the midst, they inquired, "By what power or by what name did you do this?" [8]Then Peter, filled with the Holy Spirit, said to them, "Rulers of the people and elders, [9]if we are being examined today concerning a good deed done to a cripple, by what means this man has been healed, [10]be it known to you all, and to all the people of Israel, that by the name of Jesus Christ of Nazareth, whom you crucified, whom God raised from the dead, by him this man is standing before you well. [11]This is the stone which was rejected by you builders, but which has become the head of the corner. [12]And there is salvation in no one else, for there is no other name under heaven given among men by which we must be saved."

[13]Now when they saw the boldness of Peter and John, and perceived that they were uneducated, common men, they wondered; and they recognised that they had been with Jesus. [14]But seeing the man that had been healed standing beside them, they had nothing to say in opposition. [15]But when they had commanded them to go aside out of the council, they conferred with one another, [16]saying, "What shall we do with these men? For that a notable sign has been performed through them is manifest to all the inhabitants of Jerusalem, and we cannot deny it. [17]But in order that it may spread no further among the people, let us warn them to speak no more to any one in this name." [18]So they called them and charged them not to speak or teach at all in the name of Jesus. [19]But Peter and John answered them, "Whether it is right in the sight of God to listen to you rather than to God, you must judge; [20]for we cannot but speak of what we have seen and heard." [21]And when they had further threatened

them, they let them go, finding no way to punish them, because of the people; for all men praised God for what had happened. [22]For the man on whom this sign of healing was performed was more than forty years old.

By the time Luke wrote, the separation of Christianity from the Jewish religion was complete. Paul had watched the separation and agonised over the defection of the "natural" heirs of God's promises (cf. Rom 9-11). For Luke, too, the community he belonged to was the fulfilment of the aspirations of Israel and the resurrection of Jesus inaugurated the era of the resurrection that was the characteristic hope of Israel's strictest practitioners, the Pharisees (Acts 4:2, cf. 23:6). Where Paul theologises, Luke tells the story. From its earliest days the Christian community encountered hostility from the leaders of Israel as Jesus himself had.

In the story of the arrest, interrogation and warning administered by the Sanhedrin to Peter and John, Luke narrates the first skirmish between those who "had been with Jesus" (Acts 4:13) and Israel's religious authorities, and illustrates the attitudes that initiated the process of separation. The hostility will increase in the following chapter. The reader watches the beginnings of the break with Judaism. Its momentum will gradually increase until active persecution breaks out with the death of Stephen.

The story itself warns the reader against taking it as a detailed, factual, sequential record. It is difficult to determine, for example, on what charges they were arrested or on what authority, for what reason they appear immediately before the highest court in the land. It is obvious that Luke is not reproducing details of deliberations held in camera. The factual information at his command has been subordinated to his purpose to instruct Theophilus on the origins of the Church he lives in, the function of the apostles and the essential position of the apostolic witness in the Church, as well as offering him an example of the assistance of the Holy Spirit to very ordinary men to witness fearlessly to Christ despite police action, arrest and imprisonment, and prohibition from the highest authority. In fidelity to their mission the "unlearned" apostles confront the very tribunal which condemned Jesus to death. The Spirit they have received makes them steadfast and provides the kind of wisdom that cannot be resisted, as Jesus had promised (Acts 4:14; cf. Lk 12:12; 21:15). The action is in three parts: arrest (vv.1-4), discourse of Peter (vv.5-12), and deliberation of Sanhedrin with Peter's response (vv.13-22).

Luke's Gospel has a picture of Jesus "teaching the people in the temple and proclaiming the Gospel to them" (Lk 20:2). The apostles take up, so to speak, where Jesus left off. The "teaching of the apostles" continues the teaching of Jesus just as their healing activity continues his. The difference is that they proclaim that a new era has been inaugurated by his resurrection. They provoke the indignation of the most powerful opponents imaginable, are arrested and jailed, which does not in the least impede the spread of God's word.

The teaching of Jesus had provoked the question "By what authority do you do these things?" from "the chief priests, the scribes and the elders" (Lk 20:2); now the same group puts the same question to the apostles. Peter's response is a short apologetic discourse in self-defence against the question of the Sanhedrin which leads to the proclamation of the Messiahship of Jesus attested in the Scriptures. Though similarly constructed it lacks some of the typical elements of his earlier missionary discourses. It reproduces the previous discourse in summary form, the death-resurrection antithesis appears in its simplest form, all the blame for the death of Jesus is attributed to the leaders (v.10). A different Scriptural promise (Ps 118:22) illustrates that the resurrection is the triumph of the risen Jesus over his enemies. The theme of the remission of sins is replaced by that of salvation (v.12).

The "boldness" of the apostles forces their recognition as disciples of Jesus (v.13). Boldness is a virtue highly esteemed by Luke, an endowment of the Spirit enabling the apostles to withstand external pressure in their proclamation of the word of God (e.g. Acts 4:13,29,31; 9:27,29) and helping the community to overcome internal controversies as well as all sorts of emergencies (cf. Acts 14:3). The Sanhedrin is confronted by a dilemma comparable to that in which Jesus' question about the baptism of John had placed its representatives (Lk 20:3-4). They cannot deny the miracle; the boldness of the apostles makes them "wonder," but they will not be convinced by the apostles' claim.

The apostles are given a legal admonition "not to speak or teach in this name." But this would be to disobey their mission as "witnesses" and it would deprive the community of the "teaching of the apostles" which stands at the basis of its existence (Acts 2:42). Peter's words express both absolute obedience to God and the intrinsic impossibility that these witnesses should be silent.

The response of "the people" to the teaching of the apostles parallels their response to that of Jesus (cf. Lk 20:6,19 etc.). Throughout the story of the Passion Luke has preserved a distinction between "the people" and their leaders.

In this story, the reactions of "the people" (vv.1,21) are clearly distinguished from those of "the leaders of the people" (v.8). The latter "wonder" but prohibit the apostles to teach; "the people all glorified God for what had happened" in the cure. It is the reaction of "the people" that restrains "the leaders" from more drastic action.

SUMMARY AND PRAYER. "TO SPEAK THY WORD WITH BOLDNESS." 4:23-31.

> [23]When they were released they went to their friends and reported what the chief priests and the elders had said to them. [24]And when they heard it, they lifted their voices together to God and said, "Sovereign Lord, who didst make the heaven and the earth and the sea and

everything in them, [25]who by the mouth of our father David, thy servant, didst say by the Holy Spirit,
'Why did the Gentiles rage,
and the peoples imagine vain things?
[26]The kings of the earth set themselves in array,
and the rulers were gathered together,
against the Lord and against his Anointed'—
[27]for truly in this city there were gathered together against thy holy servant Jesus, whom thou didst anoint, both Herod and Pontius Pilate, with the Gentiles and the peoples of Israel, [28]to do whatever thy hand and thy plan had predestined to take place. [29]And now, Lord, look upon their threats, and grant to thy servants to speak thy word with all boldness, [30]while thou stretchest out thy hand to heal, and signs and wonders are performed through the name of thy holy servant Jesus." [31]And when they had prayed, the place in which they were gathered together was shaken; and they were all filled with the Holy Spirit and spoke the word of God with boldness.

Luke has already given a picture of the pre-Pentecostal community at prayer (Acts 1:24-25). This tableau illustrates items of the first summary (2:42-47) such as the unity of the assembly which "lifts its voice together" as it gathers for prayer. The prayer itself is made up of a traditional address to God, a scriptural citation (Ps 2:1-2) interpreted in the light of the situation of persecution in which they find themselves, and a concluding request for present needs. A similar Old Testament prayer in time of persecution can be found in Isaiah 37:16-20.

God is addressed as "Sovereign Lord" (cf. Jer 1:6; 4:10), creator of the universe (Ps 146:6) and inspirer of the prophetic words of the Psalmist whose words anticipate the roles played in the Passion by Herod and Pilate, the Roman soldiers and the tribes of Israel. The death of Jesus, however, was guided by God's hand and his plan of salvation (cf.

Acts 2:23). Hence suffering and persecution need separate the community from fulfilling God's purpose no more than it did the Messiah. The petition is not for removal from the threats of hostile leaders but for "boldness to speak thy word" and for God's manifest assistance in its work in "healings and signs and wonders through the name of your holy Servant Jesus." Their prayer is answered in a "little Pentecost."

"ONE HEART AND SOUL." 4:32-35.

> [32]Now the company of those who believed were of one heart and soul, and no one said that any of the things which he possessed was his own, but they had everything in common. [33]And with great power the apostles gave their testimony to the resurrection of the Lord Jesus, and great grace was upon them all. [34]There was not a needy person among them, for as many as were possessors of lands or houses sold them, and brought the proceeds of what was sold [35]and laid it at the apostles' feet; and distribution was made to each as any had need.

The second summary takes up two elements of the first (2:42-47) to elaborate on the unity of the community and the position of the apostles. It first singles out their communion of mind and heart. This group fulfils the noblest human aspirations of the Hellenistic world, the ideal of friendship enshrined in slogans older than Plato and Aristotle, "friends are one heart and one soul," "the posessions of friends are common property." Luke repeats that this communion lies deeper than the pagan one, at the level of faith. It is a unity of "believers" whose sharing of goods is a sign of the deeper life they share in their faith. Thus God's promise of a time when "there will be no poor among you" (Deut 15:4) is realised in the first community which thus models both the Hellenistic ideal of friendship and the Jewish expectation of a land free of need.

This practise of the sharing of possessions is now woven into the pattern of the authority of the apostles which will be affirmed and heightened in the episodes that follow. "Filled with the Holy Spirit" (4:31) their "witness to the resurrection of the Lord Jesus" is marked by "great power," and "great grace was upon them all." In laying their possessions at the feet of the apostles the community makes a gesture of its acceptance of their authority over the new People of Yahweh.

BARNABAS.
4:36-37.

> [36]Thus Joseph who was surnamed by the apostles Barnabas (which means, Son of encouragement), a Levite, a native of Cyprus, [37]sold a field which belonged to him, and brought the money and laid it at the apostles' feet.

This short note introduces one of Luke's heroes who will feature in later crucial developments of his story, a man of impeccable Jewish credentials as a Levite yet born in the Diaspora, and illustrates the themes of the summary in a positive example. It underlines his connection with the apostles who "name" him (the name presages his future role). And Barnabas stands as an example of the community ideal of sharing of possessions.

ANANIAS AND SAPPHIRA.
5:1-11.

> **5** But a man named Ananias with his wife Sapphira sold a piece of property, [2]and with his wife's knowledge he kept back some of the proceeds, and brought only a part and laid it at the apostles' feet. [3]But Peter said,

"Ananias, why has Satan filled your heart to lie to the Holy Spirit and to keep back part of the proceeds of the land? [4]While it remained unsold, did it not remain your own? And after it was sold, was it not at your disposal? How is it that you have contrived this deed in your heart? You have not lied to men but to God." [5]When Ananias heard these words, he fell down and died. And great fear came upon all who heard of it. [6]The young men rose and wrapped him up and carried him out and buried him.

[7]After an interval of about three hours his wife came in, not knowing what had happened. [8]And Peter said to her, "Tell me whether you sold the land for so much." And she said, "Yes, for so much." [9]But Peter said to her, "How is it that you have agreed together to tempt the Spirit of the Lord? Hark, the feet of those that have buried your husband are at the door, and they will carry you out." [10]Immediately she fell down at his feet and died. When the young men came in they found her dead, and they carried her out and buried her beside her husband. [11]And great fear came upon the whole church, and upon all who heard of these things.

The story of Ananias and Sapphira is as surprising to a modern reader as anything in the New Testament. It is similar in a number of respects to Old Testament stories of drastic destruction of those who attack the holiness of God's people (e.g. Lev 10:1-3; Num 16:1-35) and to the story of Achan (Josh 7:1-26) who perished for taking what was consecrated to God. Where Luke found this story is hard to determine. It has been suggested that Luke draws on a story told to newly converted Christians to show that God watches over the purity of His People and Himself avenges its violation. Ananias and Sapphira do not "listen to" the apostles and are "cut off from the people" (cf. Acts 3:23).

By contrast with Barnabas, Ananias and Sapphira stand as a negative example both in their denial of the "one heart and soul" and in their attempt to flout the authority of

Peter. Before Ananias speaks he has already "lied to the Holy Spirit" in falsifying what is meant as a symbol of unity and submission. The power of the apostles (cf. Acts 4:33) is evident in Peter's sentence on the two sinners whose deceit appears to be a simulation of the generosity of Barnabas while retaining part of the proceeds of the sale of their property. In a Spirit-filled community a "heart filled by Satan" invites an awful fate and the sudden death of Ananias demonstrates the presence of the Spirit in a fearful way. Sapphira pays the same penalty for "tempting the Spirit of the Lord."

SUMMARY.
THE APOSTLES.
5:12-16.

> [12]Now many signs and wonders were done among the people by the hands of the apostles. And they were all together in Solomon's Portico. [13]None of the rest dared join them, but the people held them in high honour. [14]And more than ever believers were added to the Lord, multitudes both of men and women, [15]so that they even carried out the sick into the streets, and laid them on beds and pallets, that as Peter came by at least his shadow might fall on some of them. [16]The people also gathered from the towns around Jerusalem, bringing the sick and those afflicted with unclean spirits; and they were all healed.

The final summary insists on the "signs and wonders" worked not only by Peter but by "the apostles." It generalises the power Peter has just displayed and shows that the prayer of the community (4:30) has been answered. The apostles ignore the injunctions of the Sanhedrin by gathering in the Portico of Solomon. They gather "with one accord" in the Temple, objects of the awe of the people. Numbers grow, healings abound. Crowds flock from the surrounding countryside to be healed by having the shadow of Peter fall on them.

THE APOSTLES AND THE SANHEDRIN. "IF THIS PLAN IS OF GOD." 5:17-42.

[17]But the high priest rose up and all who were with him, that is, the party of the Sadducces, and filled with jealousy [18]they arrested the apostles and put them in the common prison. [19]But at night an angel of the Lord opened the prison doors and brought them out and said, [20]"Go and stand in the temple and speak to the people all the words of this Life." [21]And when they heard this, they entered the temple at daybreak and taught.

Now the high priest came and those who were with him and called together the council and all the senate of Israel, and sent to the prison to have them brought. [22]But when the officers came, they did not find them in the prison, and they returned and reported, [23]"We found the prison securely locked and the sentries standing at the doors, but when we opened it we found no one inside." [24]Now when the captain of the temple and the chief priests heard these words, they were much perplexed about them, wondering what this would come to. [25]And some one came and told them, "The men whom you put in prison are standing in the temple and teaching the people." [26]Then the captain with the officers went and brought them, but without violence, for they were afraid of being stoned by the people.

[27]And when they had brought them, they set them before the council. And the high priest questioned them, [28]saying, "We strictly charged you not to teach in this name, yet here you have filled Jerusalem with your teaching and you intend to bring this man's blood upon us." [29]But Peter and the apostles answered, "We must obey God rather than men. [30]The God of our fathers raised Jesus whom you killed by hanging him on a tree. [31]God exalted him at his right hand as Leader and Saviour, to give repentance to Israel and forgiveness of sins. [32]And we are witnesses to these things, and so is the Holy Spirit whom God has given to those who obey him."

[33]When they heard this they were enraged and wanted to kill them. [34]But a Pharisee in the council named Gamaliel, a teacher of the law, held in honour by all the people, stood up and ordered the men to be put outside for a while. [35]And he said to them, "Men of Israel, take care what you do with these men. [36]For before these days Theudas arose, giving himself out to be somebody, and a number of men, about four hundred, joined him; but he was slain and all who followed him were dispersed and came to nothing. [37]After him Judas the Galilean arose in the days of the census and drew away some of the people after him; he also perished, and all who followed him were scattered. [38]So in the present case I tell you, keep away from these men and let them alone; for if this plan or this undertaking is of men, it will fail; [39]but if it is of God, you will not be able to overthrow them. You might even be found opposing God!"

[40]So they took his advice, and when they had called in the apostles, they beat them and charged them not to speak in the name of Jesus, and let them go. [41]Then they left the presence of the council, rejoicing that they were counted worthy to suffer dishonour for the name. [42]And every day in the temple and at home they did not cease teaching and preaching Jesus as the Christ.

The final confrontation of the apostles and the Sanhedrin concludes the first part of Acts. The issue on which the story turns is made very clear by Luke. The phrase "the teaching of the apostles" recurs in one or other form almost like a refrain through the story (vv.21,26,28,42). No human power can stop this proclamation of the Good News to the people. Three groups of participants are clearly delineated. Over against "the high priests and the party of the Sadducces" (v.17) or "the council and all the senate of Israel" (v.20) stand "the apostles" and no longer Peter and John (v.18). The third group, distinct and increasingly important for Luke, exercises a decisive influence, namely "the people" (vv.20,25,26).

The narrative is dramatic and exciting. Elements of the story are customary narrative devices. "The Angel of the Lord" sets the apostles free. At precisely the time the story requires, "some one" appears to tell the Sanhedrin that the apostles are "standing in the temple and teaching the people." Deliberations held in camera are reproduced in direct speech, an appropriate address is placed on the lips of the Pharisee Gamaliel. The narrative is not without inconsistencies, such as the Sanhedrin's accepting Gamaliel's advice and acting immediately against it (v.40).

Luke deals successively with the arrest, imprisonment and liberation of the apostles (vv.17-21), the situation of the Sanhedrin (vv.21-26), the discourse of "Peter and the apostles" (vv.29-32), the advice of Gamaliel (vv.33-39), and the outcome (vv.40-42). Again Luke ascribes the opposition to the Sadducees (cf. 4:1); the counsel of restraint will come, significantly, from a Pharisee. The apostles are "filled with the Holy Spirit," their opponents "filled with jealousy."

The assembly is described in very imposing and Hellenistic terms, "all the council and all the Senate of Israel" (v.21). A delicious situation arises when the august body is reduced to perplexity by the information that all the precautions called for by the situation have naturally been observed, but somehow the prisoners cannot be found. The perplexity is heightened by "someone" who arrives to inform them that the prisoners are not only at large but busily engaged in precisely the occupation for which they had been arrested and imprisoned.

The attitude of "the people" (v.27) ensures that no violence is offered the apostles (cf. Lk 19:47-48), as they are brought to the Sanhedrin. The high priest recalls the prohibition they have disobeyed; the apostles who have witnessed to the people now witness to the leaders and indict them for the death of Jesus. The apostolic discourse (delivered by Peter and the apostles as if in unison) is comparable to the apologetic discourse of 4:8-12; its proclamation of the exaltation of Jesus introduces the title "Saviour" for the first time. While re-iterating the claim of this particular group of men to be "witnesses," the speech underlines the primacy of the witness of the Holy Spirit "given to those who obey him."

The proclamation of the apostles has led thousands of "the people" to repentance and faith. It produces the opposite effect on their leaders who want to kill the apostles (cf. Lk 19:47; Acts 5:33). This reponse is tempered by the advice of Gamaliel. His discourse (vv.35-39) refers to unsuccessful Messianic pretenders whose movements came to naught as a means of bolstering his advice to "keep away from these men and let them alone." The sequel, as Luke knows and Theophilus will see, is to show that what commenced in Jerusalem was not in any way to be confused with movements for political and national liberation, but was, indeed, a "plan of God" no human opposition could resist.

Gamaliel's advice saves the apostles from death, but not from the kind of punishment that Jesus had predicted and many missioners, including Paul, were to suffer in their missionary work among Jewish synagogues (cf. Mk 13:9; 2 Cor 11:24). The prohibition to preach is reiterated in formal terms. The apostles are beaten, but "blessed" in their "rejoicing at being counted worthy to suffer dishonour for the name" (cf. Lk 6:23). The first section closes with the apostles "teaching and preaching Jesus as the Christ." They have carried out their commission to be "witnesses in Jerusalem," in fact they have "filled Jerusalem with their teaching" (5:28). The "signs and wonders" that marked the life of Jesus are now being worked by the apostles "in the name of Jesus." With a "boldness" that is God's gift in answer to their prayers, they have witnessed both to people and to leaders. The "wonder" of many has led to numerous conversions; the "wonder" of the leaders has given way to envy.

Part II

Judea and Samaria

6:1 — 12:25

PART II
JUDEA AND SAMARIA

STEPHEN.
"FULL OF THE SPIRIT AND OF WISDOM."
6:1-7.

6 Now in these days when the disciples were increasing in number, the Hellenists murmured against the Hebrews because their widows were neglected in the daily distribution. [2]And the twelve summoned the body of the disciples and said, "It is not right that we should give up preaching the word of God to serve tables. [3]Therefore, brethren, pick out from among you seven men of good repute, full of the Spirit and of wisdom, whom we may appoint to this duty. [4]But we will devote ourselves to prayer and to the ministry of the word." [5]And what they said pleased the whole multitude, and they chose Stephen, a man full of faith and of the Holy Spirit, and Philip, and Prochorus, and Nicanor, and Timon, and Parmenas, and Nicolaus, a proselyte of Antioch. [6]These they set before the apostles, and they prayed and laid their hands upon them.

[7]And the word of God increased; and the number of the disciples multiplied greatly in Jerusalem, and a great many of the priests were obedient to the faith.

THE DEVELOPMENT of the story in chapters 6-12 extends beyond the geographical limits of Judea and Samaria, since it begins in Jerusalem and extends to

Antioch. Chapters 5-6, however, form a bridge between the first two parts of Acts; chapter 12 can be seen as a similar connection between the mission of Judea and Samaria and the move "to the ends of the earth" in the next part.

The story of the Hellenists and Stephen are the culmination of chapters 1-5 and the preparation for the move out from Jerusalem. Luke has traced the rising hostility of the leaders of the Jews from warning (4:17,21) through murderous intent (5:33) and physical violence (5:40); this culminates in the martyrdom of Stephen (7:59) and the outbreak of persecution (8:1). He has similarly developed the indictment of the Jewish leaders in the discourses of the apostles (2:23; 4:10; 5:30) which culminates in the speech of Stephen. "The blood of martyrs is the seed of Christians"; persecution forces the move out of Jerusalem and occasions the spread of the Good News to Samaria whose movement Luke traces as far as the foundations of the Church of Antioch. His picture suggests a simple and straight-forward development, a movement of the mission from Jews to Gentiles approved by the apostles and even initiated by Peter, but there are items enough in the story to show that he is simplifying a more complex historical process of growth.

Luke introduces two of the main characters of the following chapters in a story that describes a lamentably human situation in the Jerusalem community which leads to innovation in community structures at the initiative of the apostles. Before he gets to the element of persecution from outside the community he reveals internal tensions which will play a significant part in the crisis of identity provoked by the admission of the pagans.

For the first time Luke uses the term "disciples" referring to all believers (v.7). He thus parallels the situation of "believers" of a later era with those who followed Jesus during his life. Two groups are distinguished, "Hellenists" and "Hebrews." The word "Hellenist" is rare in Greek literature; it occurs only one other time in the New Testament (Acts 9:29) and is seldom attested outside it. The word "Hebrews" is uncommon in the New Testament but well attested otherwise. Attempts have been made to distinguish these groups on grounds of country of origin, mother tongue or way of life or a combination of these elements. Set in juxtaposition as here, they appear to contrast Jews who spoke different mother tongues: "Hebrews" then would be Aramaic speakers, born in Palestine, who heard the Bible read in the synagogue in Hebrew, while Hellenists would be Jews whose mother tongue was Greek, people probably born outside Palestine, who read the Bible in its Greek translation and had their own synagogues in Jerusalem. The distinction would be even sharper if "Hellenists" means Jews whose whole cultural and linguistic background was Greek. It goes without saying that these groups differed considerably in cultural and temperamental peculiarities, in their attitudes to the Gentiles, to the position of the Temple in Jewish life and to some extent, at least, even to the Law of Moses.

Friction between the two groups finds a focus in the apparently studied neglect of widows of the Hellenist group in daily distribution of relief by Hebrews. "The Twelve" (this is the only time they are designated thus in Acts) call "the body of the disciples" together, enunciate an important principle, and draw its practical conclusion for the new situation.

Two "ministries" are contrasted (v.2). The ministry of the apostles is not that of "serving on tables," the supervision of the charitable works of the community, but "prayer and the ministry of the word" in preaching and teaching. This contrast between different ministries in the community can be illustrated from the story of Martha and Mary (Lk 10:38-42). The charge to the community (v.3) is reminiscent of Moses' words prior to God's designation of Joshua as his successor (Num 27:18-23) and the advice given him by his father-in-law prior to the choice of the leaders of Israel (Ex 18:17-23). The leaders of the Hellenists are chosen by the community and appointed by the Twelve. Who imposed hands (v.6) is uncertain, whether the apostles or the whole congregation, but so far it has been the apostles who have taken the initiative in the story and received the Spirit to perform "signs and wonders" as Stephen and Philip will do. The imposition of hands is a communication of this power. Thus Moses imposed hands on his successor Joshua who received wisdom through the Spirit (Deut 34:9).

The qualities required (v.3) are excellent qualifications for relief workers but the Seven never appear in the story in this capacity. The "fullness of the Spirit," of "wisdom and faith" are the gifts which the stories of Philip and Stephen illustrate in their preaching, debating, explaining the Scriptures and evangelisation. The Seven all have Greek names, one is a convert from paganism. They were probably already leaders of the Hellenist group. By placing the story between two "growth notes" (vv.1,7) Luke suggests that a painful experience of discrimination has been changed into a situation of community growth at the initiative of the Twelve. In the conclusion (v.7) "the word of God" is practically personified. When men "obey the faith" the "word of God grows."

STEPHEN. "FULL OF GRACE AND POWER." 6:8-15.

> [8]And Stephen, full of grace and power, did great wonders and signs among the people. [9]Then some of those who belonged to the synagogue of the Freedmen (as it was called), and of the Cyrenians, and of the Alexandrians, and of those from Cilicia and Asia, arose and disputed with Stephen. [10]But they could not withstand the wisdom and the Spirit with which he spoke. [11]Then they secretly instigated men, who said, "We have heard him speak blasphemous words against Moses and God." [12]And they stirred up the people and the elders and the scribes, and they came upon him and seized him and brought him before the council, [13]and set up false witnesses who said, "This man never ceases to speak words

against this holy place and the law; [14]for we have heard him say that this Jesus of Nazareth will destroy this place, and will change the customs which Moses delivered to us." [15]And gazing at him, all who sat in the council saw that his face was like the face of an angel.

Stephen engages in debate with other Hellenistic Jews, men from the Diaspora resident in Jerusalem. He is gifted with the kind of wisdom (v.10) promised by Jesus and already evidenced by the apostles (cf. Lk 21:15). Throughout the story of his trial and death Luke paints Stephen as one who witnesses to his Master not only in his teaching but in every detail of his sufferings. His opponents arouse "the people and the elders" (the only time in Acts where the two groups share a common attitude) (cf. Lk 23:13). The accusations made against him (in two forms, vv.11,13-14) are comparable to those Luke knows were made against Jesus at his trial (cf. Mk 14:58). The witnesses may be false (v.13), but their claims highlight the significance of Stephen for Luke. He has asserted the teaching of Jesus on the transitoriness of the Temple and the abrogation of the Law and emphasized attitudes of Jesus which will make the future ministry of his people possible. God accredits him by a kind of transfiguration as he commences his speech (v.15).

STEPHEN'S SPEECH.
"YOU HAVE MURDERED THE RIGHTEOUS ONE."
7:1-53.

7 And the high priest said, "Is this so?" [2]And Stephen said:

"Brethren and fathers, hear me. The God of glory appeared to our father Abraham, when he was in Mesopotamia, before he lived in Haran, [3]and said to him, 'Depart from your land and from your kindred and go into the land which I will show you.' [4]Then he departed from the land of the Chaldeans, and lived in Haran. And after his father died, God removed him from there into this land in which you are now living; [5]yet he gave him no inheritance in it, not even a foot's length, but promised to give it to him in possession and to his posterity after him, though he had no child. [6]And God spoke to this effect, that his posterity would be aliens in a land belonging to others, who would enslave them and ill-treat them four hundred years. [7]'But I will judge the nation which they serve,' said God, 'and after that they shall come out and worship me in this place.' [8]And he gave him the covenant of circumcision. And so Abraham became the father of Isaac, and circumcised him on the eighth day; and Isaac became the father of Jacob, and Jacob of the twelve patriarchs.

[9]"And the patriarchs, jealous of Joseph, sold him into Egypt; but God was with him, [10]and rescued him out of all his afflictions, and gave him favour and wisdom before Pharaoh, king of Egypt, who made him governor over Egypt and over all his household. [11]Now there came a famine throughout all Egypt and Canaan, and great affliction, and our fathers could find no food. [12]But when Jacob heard that there was grain in Egypt, he sent forth our fathers the first time. [13]And at the second visit Joseph made himself known to his brothers, and Joseph's family became known to Pharaoh. [14]And Joseph sent and called to him Jacob his father and all his kindred, seventy-five souls; [15]and Jacob went down into Egypt. And he died, himself and our fathers, [16]and they were carried back to Shechem and laid in the tomb that Abraham had bought for a sum of silver from the sons of Hamor in Shechem.

[17]"But as the time of the promise drew near, which God had granted to Abraham, the people grew and multiplied in Egypt [18]till there arose over Egypt another king who had not known Joseph. [19]He dealt craftily with our race and forced our fathers to expose their infants, that they might not be kept alive. [20]At this time Moses was born, and was beautiful before God. And he was brought up for three months in his father's house; [21]and

when he was exposed, Pharaoh's daughter adopted him and brought him up as her own son. [22]And Moses was instructed in all the wisdom of the Egyptians, and he was mighty in his words and deeds.

[23]"When he was forty years old, it came into his heart to visit his brethren, the sons of Israel. [24]And seeing one of them being wronged, he defended the oppressed man and avenged him by striking the Egyptian. [25]He supposed that his brethren understood that God was giving them deliverance by his hand, but they did not understand. [26]And on the following day he appeared to them as they were quarrelling and would have reconciled them, saying, 'Men, you are brethren, why do you wrong each other?' [27]But the man who was wronging his neighbour thrust him aside, saying, 'Who made you a ruler and a judge over us? [28]Do you want to kill me as you killed the Egyptian yesterday?' [29]At this retort Moses fled, and became an exile in the land of Midian, where he became the father of two sons.

[30]"Now when forty years had passed, an angel appeared to him in the wilderness of Mount Sinai, in a flame of fire in a bush. [31]When Moses saw it he wondered at the sight; and as he drew near to look, the voice of the Lord came, [32]'I am the God of your fathers, the God of Abraham and of Isaac and of Jacob.' And Moses trembled and did not dare to look. [33]And the Lord said to him, 'Take off the shoes from your feet, for the place where you are standing is holy ground. [34]I have surely seen the ill-treatment of my people that are in Egypt and heard their groaning, and I have come down to deliver them. And now come, I will send you to Egypt.'

[35]"This Moses whom they refused, saying, 'Who made you a ruler and a judge?' God sent as both ruler and deliverer by the hand of the angel that appeared to him in the bush. [36]He led them out, having performed wonders and signs in Egypt and at the Red Sea, and in the wilderness for forty years. [37]This is the Moses who said to the Israelites, 'God will raise up for you a prophet from your

brethren as he raised men up.' [38]This is he who was in the congregation in the wilderness with the angel who spoke to him at Mount Sinai, and with our fathers; and he received living oracles to give to us. [39]Our fathers refused to obey him, but thrust him aside, and in their hearts they turned to Egypt, [40]saying to Aaron, 'Make for us gods to go before us; as for this Moses who led us out from the land of Egypt, we do not know what has become of him.' [41]And they made a calf in those days, and offered a sacrifice to the idol and rejoiced in the works of their hands. [42]But God turned and gave them over to worship the host of heaven, as it is written in the book of the prophets:

'Did you offer to me slain beasts and sacrifices,
forty years in the wilderness, O house of Israel?
[43]And you took up the tent of Moloch,
and the star of the god Rephan,
the figures which you made to worship;
and I will remove you beyond Babylon.'

[44]"Our fathers had the tent of witness in the wilderness, even as he who spoke to Moses directed him to make it, according to the pattern that he had seen. [45]Our fathers in turn brought it in with Joshua when they dispossessed the nations which God thrust out before our fathers. So it was until the days of David, [46]who found favour in the sight of God and asked leave to find a habitation for the God of Jacob. [47]But it was Solomon who built a house for him. [48]Yet the Most High does not dwell in houses made with hands; as the prophet says,

[49]'Heaven is my throne,
and earth my footstool.
What house will you build for me, says the Lord,
or what is the place of my rest?
[50]Did not my hand make all these things?'

[51]"You stiff-necked people, uncircumcised in heart and ears, you always resist the Holy Spirit. As your fathers did, so do you. [52]Which of the prophets did not your

> fathers persecute? And they killed those who announced beforehand the coming of the Righteous One, whom you have now betrayed and murdered, [53]you who received the law as delivered by angels and did not keep it."

Stephen's discourse to the Sanhedrin is the longest discourse in Acts. It is a missionary discourse in which Stephen proclaims Jesus as counterpart to the great figures of the past, an indictment of the leaders of Israel. The sins of Israel, constantly disobedient to the deliverers God offered and turning aside to the worship of the works of men's hands, are compounded in the readers' rejection of the prophet promised by Moses himself.

Luke has intruded this discourse into the story of the trial of Stephen. It breaks the connection of 6:8-15 with 7:55-60. It contains relatively little which can be construed as answering the charges he faces and in fact, when it does touch on them, it seems rather to confirm than to deny them (vv.35-36). Its long recitation of the history of salvation from Abraham to the foundation of the Temple is drawn principally from the Greek translation of the Pentateuch, from which it departs at a number of points to incorporate items that could well have come from Samaritan communities.

Where Luke drew the materials from which he composed this speech remains a puzzle. It was surely not from Jewish Christian sources, for he regularly uses the Greek translation of the Old Testament. All the revelations and saving deeds of God it narrates took place outside of Palestine. It seems to accept the point of view of those who accepted no other law than that received by Moses on Sinai and no other legitimate worship than that of the Tent of Testimony in the desert and rejected all that the Jewish tradition added, in particular the worship of the Jerusalem Temple. To these authors of idolatry Stephen opposes Moses, David and the prophets, rejected one after the other. Jesus is the last of these envoys, the great reformer, put to death but to return in triumph to destroy the Temple and its worship.

He commences with the story of Abraham and Joseph (vv.2-16). The discourse is a tissue of quotations from and allusions to the Old Testament, though at several points his summary differs from the details of the Genesis story. It places Abraham's vision before his migration to Haran (v.3); Gen 11:31 places it after. Stephen has Abraham leave Haran after his father's death; Gen 11:32 has his father survive for sixty years. This section of the discourse serves Stephen's purpose only in a general way by emphasizing the wandering existence of the patriarch, though it has God's promise that the posterity of Abraham will finally worship in Jerusalem (v.7, which changes Ex 3:12 from "on this mountain" to read "in this place"). With the Joseph story his purpose becomes clearer. Joseph points to Jesus (and Stephen himself) in suffering persecution because of the jealousy of his brothers. "God was with him and rescued him from his afflictions and gave him favour and wisdom" to become the providential deliverer of his brothers.

It is in the story of Moses (vv.14-43) that Luke's picture of Jesus is most transparent. Moses, "mighty in words and deeds" (v.22) is counterpart to "Jesus of Nazareth, a prophet mighty in deed and word before God and all the people" (Lk 24:19). Moses comes "to visit his brothers," to defend and avenge the oppressed. He supposes that "his brethren understood that God was giving them deliverance by his hand" (v.25) only to be thrust aside, his claim to be "ruler and judge" rejected (cf. Acts 3:15; 5:31). The picture of Moses offers an image of that of Jesus, his mission and its rejection by the Jews.

Narrative gives way to passionate indictment (vv.35-43). Moses was sent by God to his people, as Jesus was, as "ruler and deliverer" (cf. Lk 24:21; Acts 3:13), to have his claim "denied" by his people. The "signs and wonders" by which Moses set them free point to the "signs and wonders" worked by Jesus with the same saving purpose (Acts 2:22).

Moses predicted the coming of Jesus, the prophet raised up by God for his brothers (Deut 18:15; cf. Acts 3:22), and gave them "living oracles" (cf. Deut 32:45-47). His own generation "refused to obey him but thrust him aside and became Egyptian in their hearts" (v.39).

Though the story of Moses concludes here, the indictment does not. Stephen recounts Israel's worship of the golden calf, its rejoicing in "the work of its hands," its abandonment to idolatry. In an astonishing fashion he quotes the Greek translation of the prophet Amos in such a way as to have the prophet say that Israel's sacrifices in the desert were not offered to Yahweh at all but to the astral deities of the Assyrians (vv.42-43, cf. Amos 5:25-27). From its origins, the indictment runs, from the very days of its call to be the people of Yahweh, Israel rejected the true God to worship "the work of its hands."

The style again changes in v.44, returning to the tone of earlier narrative though the argument remains equally shocking to Jewish ears (vv.44-50). The portable Tent of Testimony, constructed according to a pattern dictated by God Himself, had accompanied Israel as a God-given sign of His presence during the wanderings in the desert and the victories over the Canaanites.

David wishes to "find" a simple dwelling for the God of Jacob, but Solomon built him "a house," the Temple of Jerusalem. For Stephen the Temple is comparable to the idols Israel served in the past, "the work of its hands," and in "houses made with hands," as Isaiah 66:1 makes plain; Yahweh simply does not dwell.

It is not the call for repentance but a continued indictment which concludes Stephen's speech. It is couched in the cliches of prophetic invective (cf. Ex 33:3,5; Jer 6:10; Is 63:10). He charges his judges with the crimes typical of Israel's whole career. They always "resist the Holy Spirit"; now they have crowned the persecution of the prophets of the past by their treatment of him whom the prophets foretold, "the Righteous One" (cf. Acts 3:14; 22:14), whom they have "delivered up and killed." The Law which Stephen is on trial for blaspheming simply has not been kept by his judges.

EXECUTION.
"LORD JESUS, RECEIVE MY SPIRIT."
7:54-8:1.

> [54]Now when they heard these things they were enraged, and they ground their teeth against him. [55]But he, full of the Holy Spirit, gazed into heaven and saw the glory of God, and Jesus standing at the right hand of God; [56]and he said, "Behold, I see the heavens opened, and the Son of man standing at the right hand of God." [57]But they cried out with a loud voice and stopped their ears and rushed together upon him. [58]Then they cast him out of the city and stoned him; and the witnesses laid down their garments at the feet of a young man named Saul. [59]And as they were stoning Stephen, he prayed, "Lord Jesus, receive my spirit." [60]And he knelt down and cried with a loud voice, "Lord, do not hold this sin against them." And when he had said this, he fell asleep.
> **8** [1]And Saul was consenting to his death.

The narrative is resumed from 6:14. Stephen is again "filled with the Holy Spirit" so as to perceive, in a vision, "the glory of God" and the Jesus he has proclaimed, now "exalted by God." His vision shows the claim of Jesus at his own trial fulfilled (Lk 22:69), the risen Jesus shares God's own Kingship. Ultimately it is for his confession of the risen Jesus as "Son of Man" that he dies as a blasphemer, cast outside the city and stoned. Two further items complete the parallel between the death of Jesus and the death of his witness. Jesus died commending his spirit to the Father; Stephen commends his life into the hands of Jesus "the Lord." Like his master he prays for forgiveness of his enemies, in a formalised prayer posture, kneeling and aloud. Even in his burial the disciple follows the pattern established by his Master; he is buried by "devout people" who mourn over him (cf. Lk 23:50).

In a final touch Luke introduces into the scene the figure of Saul. He is presented here as a "youth" who guards the clothes of the witnesses who stone Stephen. The sequel will show the efficacy of the prayer of the dying Stephen in the conversion of Saul and it will be Saul who continues Stephen's ministry among the Hellenists (Acts 9:29).

PERSECUTION.
"THEY WERE ALL SCATTERED."
8:1-3.

> And on that day a great persecution arose against the church in Jerusalem; and they were all scattered throughout the region of Judea and Samaria, except the apostles. [2]Devout men buried Stephen, and made great lamentation over him. [3]But Saul laid waste the church, and entering house after house, he dragged off men and women and committed them to prison.

With the death of Stephen, Luke connects the outbreak of "a great persecution against the church in Jerusalem." He makes the connection in the stereotyped phrase "on that day" and by transferring the note on Stephen's burial (v.2) from its natural position at the end of the previous story and inserting it into the beginning of the story of Saul, thus separating v.1 from v.3. His picture creates problems. Saul, who was a "young man" a few verses before, is transformed practically overnight into the embodiment of all that persecution ever meant (v.3), a strange disciple of the Gamaliel who urged entirely the opposite approach. More serious is the very selective nature of a great persecution of the Jerusalem community that leaves its leaders untouched (v.2). When he says "all were scattered," Luke is engaging in a hyperbolical flourish. In the next chapter he reports a community of disciples in Jerusalem (9:26). When he refers to "those who were scattered" (8:4; 11:19), he has in mind Philip the Hellenist and "men of Cyprus and Cyrene."

The first persecution, when it came, was aimed at men like Stephen, the Hellenists whose attitudes to the Law and the Temple must have seemed as outrageous to many other members of the community as they did to other Jews. The persecution was not general; other less aggressively evangelistic members, men and women of traditional Jewish piety, went unharmed.

Luke shows that persecution, far from impeding the Good News, is rather the providential means for scattering missioners like Philip and impels the second stage in the fulfilment of the command of the risen Lord.

PHILIP IN SAMARIA. "THEY HEARD HIM AND SAW THE SIGNS." 8:4-13.

> [4]Now those who were scattered went about preaching the word. [5]Philip went down to a city of Samaria, and proclaimed to them the Christ. [6]And the multitudes with one accord gave heed to what was said by Philip, when they heard him and saw the signs which he did. [7]For unclean spirits came out of many who were possessed, crying with a loud voice; and many who were paralysed or lame were healed. [8]So there was much joy in that city.
>
> [9]But there was a man named Simon who had previously practised magic in the city and amazed the nation of Samaria, saying that he himself was somebody great. [10]They all gave heed to him, from the least to the greatest, saying, "This man is that power of God which is called Great." [11]And they gave heed to him, because for a long time he had amazed them with his magic. [12]But when they believed Philip as he preached good news about the

> kingdom of God and the name of Jesus Christ, they were baptized, both men and women. [13]Even Simon himself believed, and after being baptized he continued with Philip. And seeing signs and great miracles performed, he was amazed.

Luke uses two stories about Philip to illustrate the spread of the Good News from Jerusalem. It is curious that the order outlined in Acts 1:8 is not followed exactly; Philip's mission in Samaria is recorded before his baptism of the eunuch in Judea. In both stories the word is received by an unexpected audience, outcasts in Jewish eyes, first by the Samaritans and then by a man who could not be part of "the assembly of Israel." These two stories are separated by Luke's insertion of another episode, the mission of Peter and John, which interrupts the first in full flight and is connected to the second by a transition which is Luke's own work (v.25).

In his first volume Luke carefully kept Jesus out of Samaritan territory, leaving its evangelisation in his orderly fashion to his second volume. Samaria has not gone entirely unnoticed, however, and Luke canonised one Samaritan in the parable of Jesus as exemplifying the commandment to love one's neighbour.

The mission of Philip is connected backwards (v.4) with persecution in Jerusalem and forwards (11:19) to the foundation of the church in Antioch, marking it out as the first step on the road from Jerusalem to Antioch. Philip is one of the scattered Hellenist missioners who "proclaim the word," or as the parallel phrase explains "preach the Christ." The city of Samaria to which he journeys is not named; it is sufficient that the Christian message passes outside the sphere of orthodox Judaism. The Samaritans were worshippers of Yahweh; they observed the law of Moses, practised circumcision, and believed in a Messianic figure to come whom they called Ta'eb, "the Returning One."

Hostility between Samaritans and Jews had a history of more than five hundred years, and it showed most clearly in their attitudes to the Temple. The Samaritans had built their own temple on Mount Gerizim which had been destroyed by the Jewish leader John Hyrcanus in 128 B.C. as a place of schismatic worship. It is not surprising, then, that Philip and others whose attitude to the Jerusalem Temple was at all similar to Stephen's might find ready refuge in Samaria.

The "crowds" (no longer, as in Jerusalem, "the people") receive the message of Philip willingly. What they "hear" is backed up by the "signs" they see. Philip performs exorcisms and cures as Jesus had promised his disciples would do and which parallel those performed by Peter (Acts 3:2). The "joy" so dear to Luke, introduced into the world by the message of the angels at Bethlehem (Lk 2:10), is communicated to the Samaritans by the message of Philip and the cures that follow in its wake (cf. Acts 13:52; 15:3).

The story of Philip and Simon the magician (vv.9-13) is the first instance in Acts of the confrontation of the Gospel with magic. The power of magic acknowledges the supremacy of the power of the Holy Spirit, operative in the "signs" Philip works. Nobody in Luke's time denied the reality of the prodigies worked by men like Simon. Things that happened in the world about them seemed at best the result of an uneasy truce between conflicting superhuman powers, malevolent and benign, on which depended the health and happiness of the individual and the stability of the social order. The sorcerer or magician who could call any of those powers by name and so bend it to his will could offer to others a cure for sickness, success in business or a love affair, domestic happiness or luck at the races. Israel had been familiar with magical practices from its earliest history. Acknowledgement of Yahweh as the one true God did not lead to the denial of other unpredictable and mighty forces but to effective acceptance of His ultimate mastery over them and His ability to bend all of them to His will for the salvation of men. But the fascination of magic remained and Israel's law proscribed such pagan practises as divination, sorcery and spiritualism (Deut 18:10).

Jesus believed in devils and saw his exorcisms as the exercise of God's Kingship subduing hostile forces (Lk 11:20). He acknowledged the power of Jewish exorcists and also the ability of pretenders to work extraordinary prodigies. Paul concedes the existence of forces that pagans call "lords" (1 Cor 8:5). He proclaimed that by raising Jesus from the dead God had established him as the "Lord" who had subdued them all.

Simon was a considerable figure in Samaria and left a well-remembered mark on its history. Justin, a century later and a Samaritan himself, records that Simon was "revered as the highest god." Other early Christian writers ascribed to him not only the heresy of Gnosticism but the origin of all heresies. According to Luke, the Samaritans were held spell-bound by him and acclaimed him as "the so-called great power of God." Philip proclaims "the kingdom of God and the name of Jesus Christ." The Samaritans come to faith one and all, Simon included. The erstwhile magician attaches himself to Philip, reduced to astonishment at the "signs and wonders" the apostle works. At this point we expect the story to continue and wonder what interesting development it is leading to when Philip simply disappears and Luke introduces Peter and John.

PETER AND JOHN.
"THAT THEY MIGHT RECEIVE THE HOLY SPIRIT."
8:14-24.

> [14]Now when the apostles at Jerusalem heard that Samaria had received the word of God, they sent to them Peter and John, [15]who came down and prayed for them that they might receive the Holy Spirit; [16]for it had not yet fallen on any of them, but they had only been baptized in the name of the Lord Jesus. [17]Then they laid their

> hands on them and they received the Holy Spirit. [18]Now when Simon saw that the Spirit was given through the laying on of the apostles' hands, he offered them money, [19]saying, "Give me also this power, that any one on whom I lay my hands may receive the Holy Spirit." [20]But Peter said to him, "Your silver perish with you, because you thought you could obtain the gift of God with money! [21]You have neither part nor lot in this matter, for your heart is not right before God. [22]Repent therefore of this wickedness of yours, and pray to the Lord that, if possible, the intent of your heart may be forgiven you. [23]For I see that you are in the gall of bitterness and in the bond of iniquity." [24]And Simon answered, "Pray for me to the Lord, that nothing of what you have said may come upon me."

If we put into direct speech the news received in Jerusalem, we can appreciate the shock of the Jewish community there. "Samaria has received the word of God!" is not only a paradox but practically a contradiction in terms. The news comes to "the apostles in Jerusalem" who send the two heroes of earlier chapters, Peter and John. The statement (v.14) is interesting for what it shows of Luke's attitude to the Petrine ministry and office in his day. Leader, spokesman, missioner in Jerusalem, object of miraculous divine care, worker of miracles parallel to those of his Master himself—Peter is nonetheless "sent" by "the apostles."

These representatives of the Jerusalem community "pray for them that they might receive the Holy Spirit." When they impose hands on them "they received the Holy Spirit." As Luke describes it this reception refers not simply to an interior renewal but to observable phenomena, which stir the wonderment of Simon and make him desire this kind of power. Peter's response (v.20) is harsh though not without biblical precedent (cf. Deut 29:18). Its emphasis falls on the "gift of God" so totally distorted when imagined as some kind of magic ritual whose secret can be bought.

Peter pronounces a form of excommunication (cf. Ps 78:37; Deut 12:12; 14:27), and follows it with a call to repentance, the first such call addressed to a non-Jew. Whereas the people in Jerusalem were invited to repent because of their part in the murder of Jesus and in preparation for his return, this short appeal is to pray that this "thought of his heart" may, if possible, be forgiven. Simon's final remark acknowledges the power of the words of Peter and John both in excommunication and in intercession with God.

The story (vv.15-17) raises the question of the relationship between the "baptism in the name of the Lord Jesus" administered by Philip, the rite of imposition of hands with prayer, and the manifest gift of the Holy Spirit in speaking in tongues and prophecy, which, in this instance, follows the imposition of hands by Peter and John.

Men and women were admitted into the community by "being baptized in the name of Jesus Christ" (Acts 2:38), "of the Lord Jesus" (Acts 8:16). The position of the baptizer is minimised, his name being mentioned only once (8:38) and Luke is at pains to say that Peter himself did not baptize (10:48) as if this ministry were not proper to an apostle. For Luke the "gift of the Spirit" is not, as Paul and John speak of the Spirit, a power of inner rebirth and renewal of the individual Christian but the Spirit that guides and indeed drives the progress of the mission of the Church as it had that of Jesus.

The relationship between baptism and the gift of the Spirit manifesting itself in observable ways, generally speaking in the gift of ecstatic utterance and inspired prophecy, is not altogether uniform in Acts. Sometimes there is no explicit mention of baptism at the entry of people into the community (4:4), on other occasions the "coming" or "falling" of the Spirit precedes the rite of initiation and is taken as a clear sign of the Spirit's intention to admit them to the rite (10:44-48), whereas for others the rite of baptism suffices to receive the gift of the Spirit. That is to say, Luke offers signs of a diversity of situations and practise in the acceptance and initiation of converts in different communities.

The story of Peter and John is parallel to that of Paul (19:1-7) in that the rite of baptism is completed by an imposition of hands by the apostles. Since after their baptism by Philip the Holy Spirit "had not fallen on any of them, they had only been baptized in the name of the Lord Jesus." Imposition of hands does not here serve the purpose of empowering or commissioning for a ministry as it did with the Seven (6:6), but brings about, by the hands of the apostles from Jerusalem, a "Samaritan Pentecost."

In the present instance this division of functions between Philip, Peter and John, is due to the arrangement of Luke. Peter and John complete the missionary initiative of Philip. They offer it authoritative sanction and recognize the communion between the Jerusalem community and the Samaritan community, thus showing a complete change in the relationship that had obtained between Jews and Samaritans for half a millenium.

PHILIP AND THE ETHIOPIAN. "HE TOLD HIM THE GOOD NEWS OF JESUS." 8:25-40.

> [25]Now when they had testified and spoken the word of the Lord, they returned to Jerusalem, preaching the gospel to many villages of the Samaritans.
>
> [26]But an angel of the Lord said to Philip, "Rise and go toward the south to the road that goes down from Jerusalem to Gaza." This is a desert road. [27]And he rose and went. And behold, an Ethiopian, a eunuch, a minister of Candace the queen of the Ethiopians, in charge of all her treasure, had come to Jerusalem to worship [28]and was returning; seated in his chariot, he was reading the prophet Isaiah. [29]And the Spirit said to Philip, "Go up and join this chariot." [30]So Philip ran to him, and heard

him reading Isaiah the prophet, and asked, "Do you understand what you are reading?" [31]And he said, "How can I, unless some one guides me?" And he invited Philip to come up and sit with him. [32]Now the passage of the scripture which he was reading was this:

"As a sheep led to the slaughter
or a lamb before its shearer is dumb,
so he opens not his mouth.
[33]In his humiliation justice was denied him.
Who can describe his generation?
For his life is taken up from the earth."

[34]And the eunuch said to Philip, "About whom, pray, does the prophet say this, about himself or about some one else?" [35]Then Philip opened his mouth, and beginning with this scripture he told him the good news of Jesus. [36]And as they went along the road they came to some water, and the eunuch said, "See, here is water! What is to prevent my being baptized?" [38]And he commanded the chariot to stop, and they both went down into the water, Philip and the eunuch, and he baptized him. [39]And when they came up out of the water, the Spirit of the Lord caught up Philip; and the eunuch saw him no more, and went on his way rejoicing. [40]But Philip was found at Azotus, and passing on he preached the gospel to all the towns till he came to Caesarea.

From the conversion of the Samaritans north of Jerusalem the story switches to the south, to Judaea and the road from Jerusalem to Gaza, the last outpost before the desert separating Judaea from Egypt. There is a great difference between the two stories about Philip. In the previous episode he is depicted as missioner and miracle worker, in this one as divinely guided explainer of the Scriptures. In Samaria his miraculous actions, astonishing enough to leave Simon astounded, are not detailed but described in a summary (8:7,13); in Judaea he is guided by very precise divine interventions and instruction to a degree equalled in no other story except that of Peter at Caesarea. In each instance, however, Philip preaches the Good News to outcasts.

The Ethiopian eunuch is on pilgrimage to Jerusalem but can never hope to be fully incorporated into the Jewish people (cf. Deut 23:1). Philip, guided by God, is on the desert road at precisely the time the eunuch is passing, approaches his chariot as the eunuch is reading precisely the Messianic passage of Is 53:7-8 concerning the Suffering Servant. A brief dialogue ensues, Philip's lines marked by a play on words (lost in English translation), the eunuch's (as befits a cultivated official) by a distinguished turn of phrase before he offers Philip precisely the opening he needs: "About whom, pray, does the prophet say this, about himself or about some one else?" Philip begins with the passage in Isaiah (used now explicitly of the death of Christ for the first time in Acts), and explains the Scriptures as "the Good News of Jesus." Providentially there is water at hand and Philip baptizes the eunuch. In this outcast who has been accepted into the people of Yahweh, who "went on his way rejoicing" to his home in the Nubian kingdom beyond Aswan on the border of Egypt, we already see the Good News making its way to "the ends of the earth."

The "Angel of the Lord" (v.26) who alternates with "the Spirit" (v.29) in instructing Philip in a way reminiscent of the alternation between the "angel of Yahweh" and "Yahweh" (e.g., Gen 16:7-14) is part of the literary machinery; Philip's activity is entirely Spirit-directed. Even his departure and subsequent arrival at Caesarea is completely guided by God. He is like Elijah (2 Kgs 2:12), transported not in a fiery chariot to heaven, but by the Spirit of the Lord on his missionary journey.

Perhaps the most instructive parallel with this story, however, is that of the journey of the risen Jesus with the two disciples to Emmaus (Lk 24:14-35), in which, "beginning with Moses and all the prophets" he taught them that "it was necessary that the Christ should suffer these things and enter into his glory" before revealing himself to them in the breaking of bread. His instruction continues through missioners whose minds have been "opened to understand the Scriptures" which, correctly understood and proclaimed, lead to faith in Jesus and Baptism.

CONVERSION OF SAUL. "HE IS A CHOSEN INSTRUMENT OF MINE." 9:1-19.

9 But Saul, still breathing threats and murder against the disciples of the Lord, went to the high priest [2]and asked him for letters to the synagogues at Damascus, so that if he found any belonging to the Way, men or women, he might bring them bound to Jerusalem. [3]Now as he journeyed he approached Damascus, and suddenly a light from heaven flashed about him. [4]And he fell to the ground and heard a voice saying to him, "Saul, Saul, why do you persecute me?" [5]And he said, "Who are you, Lord?" And he said, "I am Jesus, whom you are persecuting; [6]but rise and enter the city, and you will be told what you are to do." [7]The men who were travelling with him stood speechless, hearing the voice but seeing no one. [8]Saul arose from the ground; and when his eyes were opened, he could see nothing; so they led him by the hand and brought him into Damascus. [9]And for three days he was without sight, and neither ate nor drank.

[10]Now there was a disciple at Damascus named Ananias." And he said, "Here I am, Lord." [11]And the Lord said to him, "Rise and go to the street called Straight, and inquire in the house of Judas for a man of Tarsus named Saul; for behold, he is praying, [12]and he has seen a man named Ananias come in and lay his hands on him so that he might regain his sight." [13]But Ananias answered, "Lord, I have heard from many about this man, how much evil he has done to thy saints at Jerusalem; [14]and here he has authority from the chief priests

to bind all who call upon thy name." [15]But the Lord said to him, "Go, for he is a chosen instrument of mine to carry my name before the Gentiles and kings and the sons of Israel; [16]for I will show him how much he must suffer for the sake of my name." [17]So Ananias departed and entered the house. And laying his hands on him he said, "Brother Saul, the Lord Jesus who appeared to you on the road by which you came, has sent me that you may regain your sight and be filled with the Holy Spirit." [18]And immediately something like scales fell from his eyes and he regained his sight. Then he rose and was baptized, [19]and took food and was strengthened.

The move outwards from Jerusalem has begun with the Hellenist missioner Philip. The Samaritans and the Ethiopian eunuch are the first non-Jews to receive the word of God. Before the great initiative forced on Peter by the Holy Spirit in the admission to the Church of the household of the pagan Cornelius, Luke gets the other major figure of his cast on-stage. He has already connected Saul with the death of Stephen and drawn a cameo of the arch persecutor. Now he tells the story of his conversion and call by the risen Christ and places it on the succession of acts by which the mission to the pagans comes about through the direct guidance of God.

The importance of the episode in Luke's eyes is evident. He tells the story three times in Acts, each time at a turning point. In this chapter Paul's conversion appears in a narrative prior to the admission of the gentiles; in chapter 22 it appears in a discourse of Paul in his mother tongue to a Jerusalem crowd that brings about his rejection by the Jews, and in chapter 26 in another discourse before King Agrippa prior to his departure for Rome. The three versions differ among themselves in literary form and also in a number of details and Paul is painted differently in each. In this narrative he is described in ways that connect him with the apostles whose work he will continue. Thus the great figure of the latter half of Acts is fully introduced to the reader and his future mission sketched as their worthy successor called by the risen Jesus.

The story is in two parts, the vision of Saul (vv.1-9) and a double vision of Ananias and Saul leading to Saul's cure and baptism (vv.10-19).

"Still" (v.1) connects the story with the persecution by Saul (8:3). His "threats and murder" are elaborated in the version of his conversion in 26:10,11. "Disciples of the Lord" (vv.10,19,25,36,38) is the commonest of a wide range of synonyms for the community used in this chapter; they also "belong to the Way" (v.2 cf. 19:9,23; 22:4; 24:14,22), are "saints" (vv.13,32,41), "those who call upon thy name" (v.14), "brothers" (vv.17,30), "the church" (v.31).

Not content with persecuting the community in Jerusalem Saul seeks authority from the high priest to pursue the fleeing Christians and extradite them. He sets out in pursuit for Damascus with its large Jewish population, intent on sparing no one, neither men nor women, "to bring them bound to Jerusalem." Approaching Damascus he is suddenly enveloped with light from heaven, falls to the ground and hears a heavenly voice. The dialogue that follows is practically identical in all three accounts to which it is central.

The dialogue is constructed according to a pattern Luke found in Old Testament stories of apparitions (Gen 31:11-13; 46:2-4; Ex 3:2-10; Gen 22:1-2; 1 Sam 3:4-14). In Luke's story it is neither Yahweh nor His angel but the risen Jesus who calls Saul by name and questions him "Why do you persecute me?" Saul responds by asking what "lord" it is who has done this. The risen Jesus reveals his name. Thereby Paul learns the identity of the Lord from the risen Christ himself, and in virtue of that revelation receives his first commission, to go into Damascus. In silence he accepts his mission, the future concealed from him.

The arrival of the one-time persecutor in Damascus is a complete contrast to his departure from Jerusalem. He arrives, not indeed "bound" as he had intended his captives to arrive in Jerusalem, but blind and "led by the hand," an image of powerlessness.

A new scene commences with v.10, the vision of a Hebrew disciples named Ananias. The story of the apparition of the Lord to him in a vision is similar to that of Paul, with this difference that within the story of Ananias' vision is included a mention of another vision of Saul (v.12). Though lacking in the Old Testament this literary technique of the "double vision" is well documented in Hellenistic literature. Here it permits Luke to avoid changes of place and perspective. The risen Lord himself informs Ananias (and the reader) what has happened to Paul since his arrival in Damascus. The two visions, that of Ananias and that of Paul, correspond with one another. Paul has a vision of Ananias coming to heal him, but it is the Lord who sends Ananias to heal and baptize. The dialogue between the Lord and Ananias emphasizes the divine guidance or totally providential way in which Paul, contrary to all human expectation, was admitted to the community. Thus Ananias is given Paul's precise name and address (v.11). The understandable concern he voices underlines the terrible reputation and known intention that brings Saul to Damascus - surely that is the notorious, the one and only Saul, the arch persecutor. The response of the Lord shows the tremendous reversal that has been brought about by his action. No longer is Saul the persecutor, he is "a chosen vessel to carry my name before the Gentiles and kings and the sons of Israel." This is a programmatic utterance not unlike the commissioning of the apostles in Acts 1:8, outlining the groups before whom Paul will confess Jesus, Jews (13:5,14; 14:1 etc), gentiles (17:22; 18:6-11; 19:10) and King Agrippa (26:1-29). The words of Christ (v.16) about the sufferings Paul will have to endure counter those of Ananias (v.13) about the suffering he has inflicted. In "suffering for my name's sake" Paul will follow in the footsteps of the apostles in Jerusalem (Acts 5:41).

The story of Saul's conversion is important also because it is one point at which Luke's account can be compared with Paul's own statements. That the event had a deep and lasting effect on Paul is evident from his letters, where it is often in the background of his statements even when he is not speaking of it explicitly as he does especially in 1 Corinthians 15 and Galatians 1-2. He speaks of himself as once a fanatical persecutor of the Church (1 Cor 15:9; Gal 1:23), affirms that the Risen Christ appeared to him (1 Cor 9:1; 15:8) and connects his vocation as apostle of the Gentiles with the vision in which "God revealed His Son in me" (Gal 1:16). He even locates the episode at Damascus (Gal 1:17). If, in addition, he refers to his vision in 2 Cor 4:6 then he speaks of it in terms of light. At these decisive points Paul's epistles confirm the details of Luke's narrative, the basis of which was probably provided by Syrian and Palestinian communities who had heard it indirectly at a time when Paul was still unknown to them (cf. Gal 1:22-23).

Equally important are those points at which Luke diverges from Paul since they show us the perspective from which he is presenting his story to Theophilus. For a start Paul provides no consecutive narrative of his conversion. He mentions it infrequently and virtually only in response to attacks on the legitimacy of his message, possibly because of his aversion for visions (cf. 2 Cor 12:1-4). This makes it doubtful that Paul ever told the story of his conversion in the manner in which Luke has him do in Acts 22 and 26. Again, Luke's description of Paul's vision makes of it something less immediate than the Easter appearances of the Risen Lord to the apostles, a vision of light rather than of the person of the risen Jesus, whereas Paul himself considered it as something parallel to theirs that can be listed in one series as the last of them (1 Cor 15:3-9). In fact by Luke's earlier definition (Acts 1:21-26) Paul does not qualify as an apostle, since he did not live with Jesus; whereas on the matter of his right to the title "apostle" Paul is absolutely unequivocal: he is an apostle in virtue of a direct call from God (Gal 1:1).

Luke knew that Paul had a vision of Christ near Damascus which completely changed his life. Beyond the points in which he coincides with Paul's own remarks it is difficult to determine the extent of this information, but it is clear that much of the detail is due to Luke's own literary skill. He is showing the importance of the event for the Church, so he tells the story three times. The three accounts also give him an opportunity to answer very important questions about the right of the Church to pursue missionary activity among the pagans. How could such an orthodox Jew as Saul ever have become the missioner Paul except for the irresistible power of Christ that led him to carry out a plan intended by God?

But Luke's perspective differs from that of Paul. For Luke the "apostles" guarantee the link between the time of Jesus and that of the Church; this conception causes him problems and he later concedes the title not only to Paul but to Barnabas as well (Acts 14:4). Since he has systematically presented the interaction of the Risen Jesus with his apostles as terminating after "forty days" and culminating in Pentecost, he does not consider Paul's vision as the last of a series. As for the immediacy of Paul's call by God, it is not necessary to see Ananias as an authorised representative of the Church from whom Paul is instructed in the Gospel. He is simply one of many representatives of the Church with which Paul was in contact, all of whom recognise the legitimacy of the work he is preparing to undertake.

SAUL AT DAMASCUS.
"IN THE SYNAGOGUES . . . PROVING JESUS WAS THE CHRIST."
9:19-25.

For several days he was with the disciples at Damascus. [20]And in the synagogues immediately he proclaimed Jesus, saying, "He is the Son of God." [21]And all who

> heard him were amazed, and said, "Is not this the man who made havoc in Jerusalem of those who called on this name? And he has come here for this purpose, to bring them bound before the chief priests." [22]But Saul increased all the more in strength, and confounded the Jews who lived in Damascus by proving that Jesus was the Christ.
>
> [23]When many days had passed, the Jews plotted to kill him, [24]but their plot became known to Saul. They were watching the gates day and night, to kill him; [25]but his disciples took him by night and let him down over the wall, lowering him in a basket.

In Paul's own remarks about this period of his life, admittedly brief, but certainly clear and decisive, he says that he did not go up to Jerusalem immediately after his conversion, but into Arabia. Only "three years after," he says, "I went up to Jerusalem to visit Cephas and remained with him fifteen days. But I saw none of the other apostles except James the Lord's brother" (Gal 1:16-19). Luke's story has nothing about Paul's time in the province of Arabia. His visit to Jerusalem thus follows immediately on his conversion and first preaching in Damascus, either because Luke had no factual information about it or because he wanted to establish immediately the legitimacy of his mission by showing how it had been approved by "the apostles" in Jerusalem.

Though designated already as apostle to the Gentiles, Saul turns immediately to the synagogues. This is to be the pattern of his missionary activity. In the few days he is in the company of the disciples he preaches regularly. "Son of God" (v.20) is a title of Jesus rare in Acts (only here and 13:33) though dear to Luke himself. Here it is synonymous with "the Christ" (v.22). His hearers are amazed, Saul goes from strength to strength "proving that Jesus was the Christ." This is a feature of Paul's method - in how many synagogues did he not "prove his message from the Scriptures" (cf. Acts 28:23), and in how many synagogues did he not meet with the hostility and even murderous opposition of his audience! His first preaching sets the future pattern. He himself left Jerusalem "breathing threats and murder"; now for the first time he encounters the same murderous intent.

SAUL AT JERUSALEM. "HE WENT IN AND OUT AMONG THEM." 9:26-30.

> [26]And when he had come to Jerusalem he attempted to join the disciples; and they were all afraid of him, for they did not believe that he was a disciple. [27]But Barnabas took him, and brought him to the apostles, and declared to them how on the road he had seen the Lord, who spoke to him, and how at Damascus he had preached boldly in the name of Jesus. [28]So he went in and out among them at Jerusalem, [29]preaching boldly in the name of the Lord. And he spoke and disputed against the Hellenists; but they were seeking to kill him. [30]And when the brethren knew it, they brought him down to Caesarea, and sent him off to Tarsus.

Luke adds another touch to his portrait of Barnabas. The model of generosity (Acts 4:36-37) becomes a model of openness in introducing and recommending the very suspect Saul to "the apostles," presenting his credentials as one who has seen the Lord, spoken to him, and proclaimed his name with the same "boldness" as was shown by the apostles in Jerusalem. "He went in and out among them" (v.28); the converted persecutor enjoys the intimate companionship of the apostles as they had enjoyed that of Jesus (cf. Acts 1:21). This is the last time that the "apostles" appear as leaders of the Jerusalem church; in their final appearance in that role they set their seal of approval on the work of the man who will eventually replace them on centre stage. Saul carries on where Stephen left off, arguing with "the Hellenists" (v.29), encountering hostility as murderous in Jerusalem as at Damascus, and then returns to his native town of Tarsus.

INTERLUDE.
"THE FEAR OF THE LORD AND THE COMFORT OF THE HOLY SPIRIT."
9:31.

> [31]So the church throughout all Judea and Galilee and Samaria had peace and was built up; and walking in the fear of the Lord and in the comfort of the Holy Spirit it was multiplied.

A minor summary provides a pause between the conversion of Saul and the "acts of Peter" that will culminate in the admission of the Gentiles. "The Church" appears not as a local community but as the scattered communities as a whole. Mention of Galilee reminds us that Luke's story is deliberately selective; prior to this nothing has been said of missionary activity in Galilee. God "builds up" His Church; it responds in "fear of the Lord." After persecution, peace and "the comfort of the Holy Spirit" abound.

PETER IN JUDEA.
"JESUS CHRIST HEALS YOU."
9:32-35.

> [32]Now as Peter went here and there among them all, he came down also to the saints that lived at Lydda. [33]There he found a man named Aeneas, who had been bedridden for eight years and was paralysed. [34]And Peter said to him, "Aeneas, Jesus Christ heals you; rise and make your bed." And immediately he rose. [35]And all the residents of Lydda and Sharon saw him, and they turned to the Lord.

In the three stories that follow the reader finds himself "on circuit" with Peter in the region of the coastal plain of Palestine, first at Lydda, about 25 miles northwest of Jerusalem, then Joppa, 12 miles further, and finally at Caesarea, 30 miles further north along the coast, the administrative centre of the Romans. Luke constructs this small travel story from separate anecdotes available to him about Peter. Two miracle stories serve as prelude to the very important story about the conversion of Cornelius' household.

Verse 32 is Luke's transitional phrase; Peter is doing a pastoral visitation of various communities. The miracle story (vv. 33,34) is cut down to its essentials; the pitiful plight of the suffering Aeneas, bedridden for eight years and paralysed; Peter's word of command or healing; the immediate cure, the response of "all the residents of Lydda and Sharon" who turn to the Lord. What sets this apart from similar miracles worked by Jesus (Mk 2:1-12; Acts 3:1-9; 14:8-10) is that now Jesus continues his healing ministry through Peter.

TABITHA. "THE DEAD ARE RAISED." 9:36-43.

> [36]Now there was at Joppa a disciple named Tabitha, which means Dorcas or Gazelle. She was full of good works and acts of charity. [37]In those days she fell sick and died; and when they had washed her, they laid her in an upper room. [38]Since Lydda was near Joppa, the disciples, hearing that Peter was there, sent two men to him entreating him, "Please come to us without delay." [39]So Peter rose and went with them. And when he had come, they took him to the upper room. All the widows stood beside him weeping, and showing coats and garments which Dorcas made while she was with them. [40]But Peter put them all outside and knelt down and prayed;

then turning to the body he said, "Tabitha, rise." And she opened her eyes, and when she saw Peter she sat up. [41]And he gave her his hand and lifted her up. Then calling the saints and widows he presented her alive. [42]And it became known throughout all Joppa, and many believed in the Lord. [43]And he stayed in Joppa for many days with one Simon, a tanner.

The second miracle story is longer and more circumstantial. It resembles the story of Jesus' cure of the daughter of Jairus (Lk 8:40-42, 49-56) and the raising of a dead child to life by the prophet Elisha (2 Kgs 4:32-37). Tabitha, a widow "full of good works and alms that she gave" (in Luke's language no mean praise), has died and is prepared for burial. The disciples send for Peter who is at Lydda. When he arrives Dorcas' generosity is displayed in a wordless demonstration of clothes she has made for others. The repetition (v.40) of phrases from the story of Elisha show Peter as a successor of the Old Testament prophet. After prayer Peter speaks a word of command practically identical with that of Jesus in the parallel miracle of Jairus' daughter (cf. Mk 5:41; Lk 8:54) and she is restored to life. The result of the second miracle, as of the first, is that "many believed in the Lord." Peter lodges with Simon, a tanner whose trade was generally regarded as defiling or impure, an association that perhaps shows an attitude to outcasts similar to that of Jesus and which will develop into something much greater in the story that follows.

PETER AND THE PAGANS:
SCENE ONE, CAESAREA.
"SEND . . . AND BRING ONE SIMON."
10:1-8.

10 At Caesarea there was a man named Cornelius, a centurion of what was known as the Italian Cohort, [2]a devout man who feared God with all his household,

> gave alms liberally to the people, and prayed constantly to God. [3]About the ninth hour of the day he saw clearly in a vision an angel of God coming in and saying to him, "Cornelius." [4]And he stared at him in terror, and said, "What is it, Lord?" And he said to him, "Your prayers and your alms have ascended as a memorial before God. [5]And now send men to Joppa, and bring one Simon who is called Peter; [6]he is lodging with Simon, a tanner, whose house is by the seaside." [7]When the angel who spoke to him had departed, he called two of his servants and a devout soldier from among those that waited on him, [8]and having related everything to them, he sent them to Joppa.

The sequence that begins with Cornelius the Roman centurion in Caesarea and ends with Peter defending his actions in Jerusalem is a series of seven connected scenes, which constitute the longest of the stories in Acts, a matter of 66 verses (excluding flashbacks in 15:7-9,14) as against a total of 58 for the three stories of Paul's conversion and 41 for the Pentecost story including the discourse of Peter.

The length of the sequence indicates its importance to Luke. What happens at Caesarea leads to the authoritative decision that he ascribes to the "Council of Jerusalem." The lessons of this episode are decisive in the formulation of the principle enunciated by James: "From the beginning God has taken care to draw from the pagans a people for His name" (15:14). In this story the pagans aspire to enter God's people, represented by the Jerusalem community, which ultimately will communicate to them what it had itself received (10:36-42). In their entry the promises of God are fulfilled (10:43 cf. 15:14,16). From now on the pagans are in the forefront. The events at Caesarea are central in another way. The missionary activity that commenced with the persecution in the work of Philip in Samaria and Judea continues from 11:19, but now missioners move out to the pagans. The Caesarea story with its conclusion in Jerusalem has been placed in the centre of this missionary activity and the initiative in the reception of the pagans comes from God through no less a figure than Peter.

The story touches on the two basic problems involved in the admission of the Gentiles. What seems most fundamental was whether pagans could be admitted into the "holy" community without being obliged to the law of Moses. To offer the good things of the promised Messianic era to uncircumcised pagans was to affirm the independence of Christianity from Judaism. This might not have seemed so striking in the case of a "god-fearing" pagan like Cornelius, attached to the Jewish cult and creed, but his case was the thin end of the wedge. The second problem that is documented not only in Acts but in the epistles of Paul is whether contact with a gentile Christian, particularly acceptance of hospitality from and sharing of the same table, would defile a Jewish Christian. Luke's story provides answers to both of these problems. What happens in Antioch after the breakthrough in Caesarea amounts to the foundation of a new community of a universal type by an "alliance" between Jews and pagans which will automatically involve table fellowship.

It is clear that Luke had information that he was using. An accumulation of words never used elsewhere, difficulties of Greek syntax, breaks or inconsistencies in the story all show that he was imposing his pattern on his sources. The length of the sequence is largely due to his systematic use of repetition (cf. 11:5-17 with 10:1-48, inside 10:1-48 the vision of Cornelius is described three times, as is the sending of envoys), to his use of the device of the double vision (much more elaborate than in the story of Paul's conversion), and his insertion of a discourse he ascribes to Peter which can be easily detached from the context and was independent in origin from the rest of the story.

Through all this what Luke makes inescapably clear is that the admission of the Gentiles at Caesarea was due entirely to the initiative of God who presided over events whose meaning was only gradually made clear to the participants. The Spirit it was who brought about the encounter between Peter and Cornelius to renew for the pagans the miracle of Pentecost. Authoritative figure that he was, Peter's role was one of obedience and acceptance, of reflection on the events as they unfolded.

Cornelius is a centurion, part of the garrison in Caesarea, a "god-fearing man" or devout Gentile who attended synagogue worship, espoused Jewish monotheism and its moral code without being circumcised or observing the dietary laws, the latter at least being impossible in the case of a soldier. He is a prayerful, alms-giving man. In a vision this pagan is assured that his prayers and alms have been as pleasing to God as a Jewish sacrifice (cf. Lev 2:2,9,16). Like Ananias he is given the precise name and address at which he can find a man whom he is to invite to his house. Nothing further is revealed to him; he sends two of his household and a soldier devout as himself.

PETER AND THE PAGANS: SCENE TWO, JOPPA. "WHAT GOD HAS CLEANSED . . ." 10:9-16.

> [9]The next day, as they were on their journey and coming near the city, Peter went up on the housetop to pray, about the sixth hour. [10]And he became hungry and desired something to eat; but while they were preparing it, he fell into a trance [11]and saw the heaven opened, and something descending, like a great sheet, let down by four corners upon the earth. [12]In it were all kinds of animals and reptiles and birds of the air. [13]And there came a voice to him, "Rise, Peter; kill and eat." [14]But Peter said, "No, Lord; for I have never eaten anything that is common or unclean." [15]And the voice came to him again a second time, "What God has cleansed, you must not call common." [16]This happened three times, and the thing was taken up at once to heaven.

As these envoys of Cornelius are nearing the end of their overnight journey, Peter prays, as his master had done before the great turning points in his life. Hungry as he is he falls into ecstasy, perceiving things in an entirely different way. He is given a glimpse into heaven, from which comes "an object" or "vessel" like a great sheet (the word can mean cloth, sail cloth, table cloth, veil or tent). Some of the details of his vision are reminiscent of the vision of Ezechiel, as is his reply "Never, Lord" (cf. Ezek 4:14). Either the "object" is simply a receptacle for the items on a heavenly menu to settle the hunger he feels, or it is a kind of descending tent suggesting the divine sanctuary where God speaks in a hidden manner in view of a striking happening about to take place. The menu (v.12) consists of all the animals of creation (cf. Gen 1:24).

Peter's understanding of the vision comes in stages. He is instructed not to regard anything God has made clean as something that will defile him. Three times he is invited to eat of all these animals. Three times he refuses, three times his refusal is rejected.

PETER AND THE PAGANS: SCENE THREE, JOPPA. "HOSPITALITY TO PAGANS." 10:17-23.

[17]Now while Peter was inwardly perplexed as to what the vision which he had seen might mean, behold, the men that were sent by Cornelius, having made inquiry for Simon's house, stood before the gate [18]and called out to ask whether Simon who was called Peter was lodging there. [19]And while Peter was pondering the vision, the Spirit said to him, "Behold, three men are looking for you. [20]Rise and go down, and accompany them without hesitation; for I have sent them." [21]And Peter went down to the men and said, "I am the one you are looking for; what is the reason for your coming?" [22]And they said, "Cornelius, a centurion, an upright and God-fearing

man, who is well spoken of by the whole Jewish nation, was directed by a holy angel to send for you to come to his house, and to hear what you have to say." [23]So he called them in to be his guests.

The Spirit leads Peter further. While Peter is perplexed as to what the vision means, the envoys of Cornelius arrive at the house of Simon and ask for help. The Spirit instructs Peter to accompany them, for their coming is His work. The vision of Cornelius offers some further light to him; he is to come to the house of Cornelius there to speak to pagans. Peter takes a further step by inviting the pagans into the house of Simon as his guests.

PETER AND THE PAGANS: SCENE FOUR, CAESAREA. "GOD HAS SHOWN ME . . ." 10:23-33.

The next day he rose and went off with them, and some of the brethren from Joppa accompanied him. [24]And on the following day they entered Caesarea. Cornelius was expecting them and had called together his kinsmen and close friends. [25]When Peter entered, Cornelius met him and fell down at his feet and worshipped him. [26]But Peter lifted him up, saying, "Stand up; I too am a man." [27]And as he talked with him, he went in and found many persons gathered; [28]and he said to them, "You yourselves know how unlawful it is for a Jew to associate with or to visit any one of another nation; but God has shown me that I should not call any man common or unclean. [29]So when I was sent for, I came without objection. I ask then why you sent for me."

[30]And Cornelius said, "Four days ago, about this hour, I was keeping the ninth hour of prayer in my house; and behold, a man stood before me in bright apparel, [31]saying, 'Cornelius, your prayer has been heard and your

alms have been remembered before God. [32]Send therefore to Joppa and ask for Simon who is called Peter; he is lodging in the house of Simon, a tanner, by the seaside.' [33]So I went to you at once, and you have been kind enough to come. Now therefore we are all here present in the sight of God, to hear all that you have been commanded by the Lord."

Peter sets out accompanied by "some of the brethren from Joppa" who will be witnesses of the events and able to confirm Peter's testimony (11:12). Cornelius offers Peter a welcome befitting a heavenly messenger, as indeed an apostle coming to proclaim God's word is, but Peter refuses the honours. Entering the house of a pagan is a further step along his Spirit-guided way. The deepest meaning of his vision has been made clear; it is not only that the distinction between clean and unclean foods has been abolished by God, so also has the distinction between Jews and Gentiles. At the Council of Jerusalem he will explain more explicitly the lesson he has learned, that God "made no distinction between us and them, but purified their hearts by faith" (15:9). But this lesson comes after further events. With ideal dispositions the pagans await "before God to hear all that you have been commanded by the Lord."

PETER AND THE PAGANS: SCENE FIVE, CAESAREA. "PETER'S SPEECH." 10:34-43.

[34]And Peter opened his mouth and said: "Truly I perceive that God shows no partiality, [35]but in every nation any one who fears him and does what is right is acceptable to him. [36]You know the word which he sent to Israel, preaching good news of peace by Jesus Christ (he is Lord of all), [37]the word which was proclaimed

> throughout all Judea, beginning from Galilee after the baptism which John preached: [38]how God anointed Jesus of Nazareth with the Holy Spirit and with power; how he went about doing good and healing all that were oppressed by the devil, for God was with him. [39]And we are witnesses to all that he did both in the country of the Jews and in Jerusalem. They put him to death by hanging him on a tree; [40]God raised him on the third day and made him manifest; [41]not to all the people but to us who were chosen by God as witnesses, who ate and drank with him after he rose from the dead. [42]And he commanded us to preach to the people, and to testify that he is the one ordained by God to be judge of the living and the dead. [43]To him all the prophets bear witness that every one who believes in him receives forgiveness of sins through his name."

Peter's discourse to the pagans in the house of Cornelius is the last example Luke offers of the preaching of the apostles as leaders of the Jerusalem church. In his last missionary discourse Peter finally addresses a pagan audience. The discourse shows signs of Luke's own editorial hand, for example, the awkward phrase "he is Lord of all" (v.36) welding the discourse to its context, and some characteristic phrases (v.38) and themes (v.41) in which he is interested. But the discourse also emphasizes themes that otherwise receive no special attention from Luke and probably originated in the instruction given to the pagan converts in Palestine, people not yet acquainted with the Gospel story but aware of the polemic between the Church and the Synagogue. Luke edits his sources to construct a discourse of Peter showing how the Gospel is to be extended beyond the Jewish people to whom it was originally offered to make the gifts of the Messianic era available to every believer.

It was an item of Jewish faith that "The Lord your God . . . is not partial and takes no bribes" (Deut 10:17). Peter's experience has led him to understand the deepest meaning of that phrase; God's impartiality extends beyond the Jewish people so that "in any nation any one who fears him and practises righteousness is acceptable to him."

What follows from this point is not particularly adapted to the situation of Peter's audience, and the "you know" (v.37) is better understood as directed to Luke's readers than to Peter's hearers. "The Word" (v.36) refers to the preaching of the "good news of peace through Jesus Christ" by the apostles, sent first to "the sons of Israel." This does not gainsay the fact, Peter adds in an unwieldy parenthesis, that Jesus is Lord of pagans as well as Jews.

The summary of Jesus' ministry (vv.37-39) refers to the baptism of Jesus by John as an anointing "with the Holy Spirit and with power," the way Luke presents the ministry of Jesus in the Gospel (cf. Lk 4:14,18-19) namely as a fulfilment of the prophecy of Isaiah 61:1-2. However the remark that "he went about doing good and healing all that were oppressed by the devil" is not an aspect of Jesus' ministry strongly emphasized by Luke nor is his role as future judge of the living and the dead. By contrast with earlier discourses addressed to Jewish audiences, the indictment of the Jews is lacking and the death of Jesus is described in the terms of Deuteronomy (21:23) as the curse God reversed in raising him from the dead.

A characteristic item of this discourse is its insistence on the role of the apostles as witnesses. The statement itself is not unusual (cf. 2:32; 5:32) but the contrast "not to all the people but to us who were chosen by God as witnesses" seems to be an answer to a question that must have been asked by Jewish opponents many times from the earliest days; "why is it that so few and such undistinguished men have actually seen the Jesus they claim is alive?" Ultimately it was a matter of God's choice, but their fellowship with the risen Christ, Luke adds, carried with it a commission to preach to the people and to testify to Jesus as judge of the living and the dead.

Other discourses adduce precise Scriptural proof for their assertions; but here the concluding reference is quite general. The finale (v.43) differs significantly from anything that precedes it in claiming that the prophets bear witness that "*every one* who believes in him receives forgiveness of sins through his name."

PETER AND THE PAGANS: SCENE SIX, CAESAREA. "THE PENTECOST OF THE PAGANS." 10:44-48.

> [44]While Peter was still saying this, the Holy Spirit fell on all who heard the word. [45]And the believers from among the circumcised who came with Peter were amazed, because the gift of the Holy Spirit had been poured out even on the Gentiles. [46]For they heard them speaking in tongues and extolling God. Then Peter declared, [47]"Can any one forbid water for baptizing these people who have received the Holy Spirit just as we have?" [48]And he commanded them to be baptized in the name of Jesus Christ. Then they asked him to remain for some days.

While they are "hearing the word" the Holy Spirit comes on the pagans. The Jewish Christians accompanying Paul respond with the same amazement as the people of Jerusalem to the original coming of the Holy Spirit at Pentecost (cf. 2:7,12), but the amazement is due to their realization that "the gift of the Spirit has been poured out even on the pagans." Their ecstatic utterance, "speaking in tongues and extolling God" forces Peter to the conclusion that "they have received the Holy Spirit as we did" and raises the question "can anyone forbid water for baptizing these people" in a case where the Holy Spirit has so clearly taken the initiative. Peter has offered hospitality to pagans, has gone into Cornelius' house and finally accepts the offer of hospitality made to him by a pagan.

PETER AND THE PAGANS: SCENE SEVEN, JERUSALEM. "EVEN THE GENTILES . . ." 11:1-18.

11 Now the apostles and the brethren who were in Judea heard that the Gentiles also had received the word of God. [2]So when Peter went up to Jerusalem, the circumcision party criticised him, [3]saying, "Why did you go to uncircumcised men and eat with them?" [4]But Peter began and explained to them in order: [5]"I was in the city of Joppa praying; and in a trance I saw a vision, something descending, like a great sheet, let down from heaven by four corners; and it came down to me. [6]Looking at it closely I observed animals and beasts of prey and reptiles and birds of the air. [7]And I heard a voice saying to me, 'Rise, Peter; kill and eat.' [8]But I said, 'No, Lord; for nothing common or unclean has ever entered my mouth.' [9]But the voice answered a second time from heaven, 'What God has cleansed you must not call common.' [10]This happened three times, and all was drawn up again into heaven. [11]At that very moment three men arrived at the house in which we were, sent to me from Caesarea. [12]And the Spirit told me to go with them, making no distinction. These six brethren also accompanied me, and we entered the man's house. [13]And he told us how he had seen the angel standing in his house and saying, 'Send to Joppa and bring Simon called Peter; [14]he will declare to you a message by which you will be saved, you and all your household.' [15]As I began to speak, the Holy Spirit fell on them just as on us at the beginning. [16]And I remembered the word of the Lord, how he said, 'John baptized with water, but you shall be baptized with the Holy Spirit.' [17]If then God gave the same gift to them as he gave to us when we believed in the Lord Jesus Christ, who was I that I could withstand God?" [18]When they heard this they were silenced. And they glorified God, saying, "Then to the Gentiles also God has granted repentance unto life."

The story is not yet finished. The Jerusalem community and other communities in Judaea hear the news. Peter is criticised by "those of the circumcision" (v.2), in this case the community as a whole. Criticism of the Petrine ministry is thus firmly established as current in apostolic times, even, though Luke does not say so explicitly, by Peter's brother apostles.

Peter's discourse (vv.4-17) differs in tone and purpose from the missionary discourse that precedes it. As with other such apologetic discourses the self defence of the speaker responds to wider issues than the one which prompts it. Criticism has been aimed at Peter's acceptance of hospitality from the pagans; his response is more comprehensive and raises the matter of their baptism. It is the third time the reader has heard the story of Peter's vision and the second time he has heard the story of the coming of the Spirit on the pagans and their baptism. There are some variations in detail. Peter's words are words of "salvation" for Cornelius and his house (v.14), the Holy Spirit comes on the pagans as Peter began to speak (v.15) highlighting its suddenness all the more, the connexion with Pentecost is underlined in Peter's addition of the phrase "as upon us in the beginning" (v.17). It is not without purpose that Luke repeats Peter's earlier question "who was I that I could withstand God?" (v.17).

ANTIOCH.
"THE DISCIPLES WERE FOR THE FIRST TIME CALLED CHRISTIANS."
11:19-26.

> [19]Now those who were scattered because of the persecution that arose over Stephen travelled as far as Phoenicia and Cyprus and Antioch, speaking the word to none except Jews. [20]But there were some of them, men of Cyprus and Cyrene, who on coming to Antioch spoke to the Greeks also, preaching the Lord Jesus. [21]And the

> hand of the Lord was with them, and a great number that believed turned to the Lord. [22]News of this came to the ears of the church in Jerusalem, and they sent Barnabas to Antioch. [23]When he came and saw the grace of God, he was glad; and he exhorted them all to remain faithful to the Lord with steadfast purpose; [24]for he was a good man, full of the Holy Spirit and of faith. And a large company was added to the Lord. [25]So Barnabas went to Tarsus to look for Saul; [26]and when he had found him, he brought him to Antioch. For a whole year they met with the church, and taught a large company of people; and in Antioch the disciples were for the first time called Christians.

Luke has devoted so much space and artistic attention to the Caesarea episode that the notes he writes on the origin of the Church in Antioch come as something of an anti-climax. We expect something more elaborate when the Gospel arrives in the third greatest city of the Roman world after Alexandria and Rome, for it is here that the distinctive face of the community is revealed so that pagans, only too familiar with both the pagan and Jewish religion, are obliged to coin the name so proudly born by the Church throughout its history. It might be thought, too, that here Luke could document his story directly from the records of the great missionary centre, but it is not at all certain that the material he uses for his picture derives from local recollection. Even if it does, the familiar phraseology of Luke shows that he has, as usual, incorporated it carefully into his own pattern.

The origins of the church in Antioch are a providential result of the persecution of the Church in Jerusalem; 11:19 takes up from 8:1,4. Hellenist missioners have worked their way north along the coast of Palestine through Phoenicia to Antioch, others have crossed to Barnabas' homeland in Cyprus. Antioch was twenty eight miles inland along the Orontes from its port, Seleucia, which placed the metropolis in contact with every Mediterranean harbour. Caravan routes linked it with the interior, beyond the Euphrates as far as India. Its temple of Apollo and groves of Daphne were well known. No longer capital of the Seleucid empire it was, nonetheless, the seat of the Roman governor of Syria and its population included many Jews.

Luke marks out two phases in the missionary initiative. The first is the proclamation of the word to Jews alone. In the second, "men of Cyprus and Cyrene" on arriving in Antioch "spoke to the Greeks also, preaching the Lord Jesus" (v.20). The Greeks in question are no longer "Hellenists" or Greek-speaking Jews, nor are they "god-fearing men," pagans attached to the synagogue and Judaism like Cornelius, but uncircumcised pagans. In the briefest of phrases Luke notes a momentous change in missionary tactics implying a revolutionary change of attitude to the very identity of the community. The hindsight of half a century permits his judgment that "the great number that believed" and "turned to the Lord" shows God's approval and assistance of their efforts.

"The Lord" that the pagans "turned to" was the risen Jesus. The title "Kyrios" had been current in Asia Minor and Hellenistic lands as an honorific title for gods and kings from 100 B.C.; from 30 B.C. it was applied to Roman emperors. Hellenist missioners would have become accustomed to it in Palestine, especially in the Eucharistic acclamation "Come, Lord Jesus" (cf. 1 Cor 16:22), where it suggested Jesus' rank as Messianic king, God's plenipoteniary, wielding His divine power. In the Hellenistic world they entered in Antioch it acquired other overtones, expressing the unique claim of Jesus to divine rank, honour and obedience over against any person or cosmic force that had ever been designated "lord" (cf. 1 Cor 8:5). "Turning to" the Lord Jesus would also mean a "turning from" any other claimant to the title.

The Church of Antioch is perhaps best envisaged as a gathering of small domestic communities linked by bonds of charity, gathering frequently in more or less plenary sessions, some of the groups Jewish Christians while others, born of the activity of the men like those from "Cyprus and Cyrene," were composed of converted pagans.

Like Samaria (9:14), Antioch, too, receives its visitor from the mother community of Jerusalem. Barnabas is not, as yet anyway, graced with the title "apostle" though he is "sent" (v.22). What has already been said about him has laid the ground for this further detail of Luke's portrait. His name has been explained as "son of encouragement" (4:36) and this is the ministry he exercises, "encouraging them to remain faithful to the Lord with steadfast purpose" (v.23). So his approbation of the Church of Antioch comes from "a good man, full of the Holy Spirit and of faith." His previous recommendation of the persecutor Saul to the Jerusalem community (8:27) is followed through by a journey to Tarsus and his invitation to Saul to come and work with him in Antioch (v.26).

The title "Christians" shows that the pagans regarded "Christ" as a proper name. They choose what is distinctive of this unprecedented grouping of Jews and pagans. In Antioch the real foundation of the Church is laid bare - not Moses or the Law or worship in the Jerusalem Temple, but faith in Jesus Christ.

"RELIEF TO THE BRETHREN WHO LIVED IN JUDEA." 11:27-30.

> [27]Now in these days prophets came down from Jerusalem to Antioch. [28]And one of them named Agabus stood up and foretold by the Spirit that there would be a great famine over all the world; and this took place in the days of Claudius. [29]And the disciples determined, every one according to his ability, to send relief to the brethren who lived in Judea; [30]and they did so, sending it to the elders by the hand of Barnabas and Saul.

The mother community has offered its approval by the encouragement and continued missionary activity of Barnabas. Now some of its prophets visit Antioch. In consequence of their prophetic warning of impending famine the Antioch community strengthens its connection with Jerusalem by sending a relief mission headed by Barnabas and Saul.

Acts provides a whole gallery of prophetic figures and ascribes a wide range of functions to them. The preaching of the apostles, their teaching, interpretation of current events in the light of the Scriptures, particularly in their application to the life, death and resurrection of Jesus, the miraculous cure of Tabitha, the "encouragement" of Barnabas - all these are manifestations of the prophetic Spirit given at Pentecost as are the ecstatic praise of God by Samaritans and pagans. Agabus predicts "a great famine over all the world," which happened, Luke explains, in the reign of Claudius. This chronological note hardly pinpoints the occasion; Claudius reigned between the years 41 A.D. - 54 A.D. The collection is sent not to "the apostles" but to "the elders," a group in the Jerusalem Church who appear here for the first time.

It is hard to place this second visit of Paul to Jerusalem mentioned in Acts, since it cannot be checked against Paul's writings where it is not mentioned.

PERSECUTION IN JERUSALEM.
THE DEATH OF JAMES.
12:1-5.

> **12** About that time Herod the king laid violent hands upon some who belonged to the church. [2]He killed James the brother of John with the sword; [3]and when he saw that it pleased the Jews, he proceeded to arrest Peter also. This was during the days of Unleavened Bread. [4]And when he had seized him, he put him in prison, and delivered him to four squads of soldiers to guard him,

intending after the Passover to bring him out to the people. [5]So Peter was kept in prison; but earnest prayer for him was made to God by the church.

Framed within the relief mission of Barnabas and Paul is the story of the persecution of the Jerusalem community. Whereas in chapter 5 the apostles were miraculously spared through the intervention of Gamaliel, this time James the son of Zebedee is put to death. It is not his martyrdom, however, that Luke concentrates on, but on the deliverance of Peter, due to the wonderful intervention of the Lord.

Set off against Peter is King Herod, who seeks to put the apostle to death and in his pride dies himself the typical death of the persecutor. Where did Luke get the materials for this story? The circumstances of the death of Herod were well known; the story as told by Josephus is similar in some details to Luke's. The first martyrdom of an apostle was surely remembered long after, and the stories of the deliverance of Peter and his reunion with the community seem to ante-date Luke, who nonetheless uses them to serve his own purpose.

With the exception of the parallel miracle worked in favour of Paul, there is nowhere in Acts where the marvellous is so accented as in this story. "The angel of the Lord" takes the initiative at every stage in Peter's deliverance and it is to his intervention that the death of Herod is directly ascribed. Luke's story of Peter's escape is no videotape replay as some of its own remarks suggest; it is a story told after the manner of known stories of wondrous escapes in Hellenistic literature. In the manner appreciated by his audience Luke tells the story of the watch the Lord keeps over His Church, how he answers its prayers for help in ways it finds hard to believe.

"About that time" (v.1) refers to the relief mission of Barnabas and Saul (11:30; 12:25). "Herod the King" is Herod Agrippa I, grandson of Herod the Great (though endowed with little of his energy) and friend of the emperor

Caligula to whom he owed his crown. He ruled over the northern territories he inherited from his uncle Philip until 41 A.D. and then over Judea, Samaria and Idumaea as well. He favoured the Pharisees although he was a devotee of Hellenistic culture. "James the brother of John" is the first of the apostles to be put to death. His martyr's death does not impede his role as leader of eschatological Israel, hence, unlike Judas, no replacement is needed.

Whether this persecution touched others Luke does not say, nor does he delay over the martyrdom of James as he did over that of Stephen. He passes on to the story of Peter as an example of the Lord's wonderful care for his own. Peter is arrested and imprisoned in custody of four soldiers.

PETER'S ESCAPE. "THE LORD HAS SENT HIS ANGEL AND SAVED ME." 12:6-11.

> [6]The very night when Herod was about to bring him out, Peter was sleeping between two soldiers, bound with two chains, and sentries before the door were guarding the prison; [7]and behold, an angel of the Lord appeared, and a light shone in the cell; and he struck Peter on the side and woke him, saying, "Get up quickly." And the chains fell off his hands. [8]And the angel said to him, "Dress yourself and put on your sandals." And he did so. And he said to him, "Wrap your mantle around you and follow me." [9]And he went out and followed him; he did not know that what was done by the angel was real, but thought he was seeing a vision. [10]When they had passed the first and the second guard, they came to the iron gate leading into the city. It opened to them of its own accord, and they went out and passed on through one street; and immediately the angel left him. [11]And Peter came to himself, and said, "Now I am sure that the Lord has sent his angel and rescued me from the hand of Herod and from all that the Jewish people were expecting."

The scene opens with Peter under heavy guard in jail and the Church in earnest prayer. Security precautions are doubled: two guards, two chains, sentries between prison door and impassable iron outer gate. "The angel of the Lord" appears. A completely passive Peter is prodded in the ribs, wakened, and the chains fell away. The Angel even supervises and directs the very simple stages of his dressing! Following the angel as if in a dream Peter negotiates the hazards of the sentries; as to the great main gate it simply swings open of its own accord. A street away from the jail "the Angel left him.." In the concluding verse Luke instructs the reader as to the meaning of the episode - Peter's wonderful deliverance is due entirely to the Lord.

REUNION.
"THE LORD BROUGHT HIM OUT OF PRISON."
12:12-17.

> [12]When he realised this, he went to the house of Mary, the mother of John whose other name was Mark, where many were gathered together and were praying. [13]And when he knocked at the door of the gateway, a maid named Rhoda came to answer. [14]Recognising Peter's voice, in her joy she did not open the gate but ran in and told that Peter was standing at the gate. [15]They said to her, "You are mad." But she insisted that it was so. They said, "It is his angel!" [16]But Peter continued knocking; and when they opened, they saw him and were amazed. [17]But motioning to them with his hand to be silent, he described to them how the Lord had brought him out of the prison. And he said, "Tell this to James and to the brethren." Then he departed and went to another place.

After deliverance comes reunion with the community. Peter comes to his senses to seek the group gathered in prayer for him at the house of Mary, mother of John Mark (Luke thus introduces another of his cast of characters who will feature in future episodes beginning with 12:25).

In a comic episode the prison escapee stands knocking at the door in the middle of the night while the portress, unable to believe her ears, rushes into the earnest prayer meeting to announce that their prayers have been answered and that Peter is at the door! This kind of answer to prayer is too much for the devout assembly which promptly brands it as madness. When finally Peter is admitted his response to their wonderment is to explain "how the Lord brought him out of prison." Luke has reinforced his lesson beyond the incomprehension of even the dullest reader.

In one of the shortest exit lines in literature Peter instructs them to "tell this to James and the brethren" before he departs "to another place," completely unspecified, to make his definitely last appearance at the Council of Jerusalem. From this point James appears as the leader of the Jerusalem community.

HEROD'S DEATH. "BECAUSE HE DID NOT GIVE GOD THE GLORY." 12:18-23.

> [18]Now when day came, there was no small stir among the soldiers over what had become of Peter. [19]And when Herod had sought for him and could not find him, he examined the sentries and ordered that they should be put to death. Then he went down from Judea to Caesarea, and remained there.
>
> [20]Now Herod was angry with the people of Tyre and Sidon; and they came to him in a body, and having persuaded Blastus, the king's chamberlain, they asked for peace, because their country depended on the king's country for food. [21]On an appointed day Herod put on his royal robes, took his seat upon the throne, and made an oration to them. [22]And the people shouted, "The voice of a god, and not of man!" [23]Immediately an angel of the Lord smote him, because he did not give God the glory; and he was eaten by worms and died.

The story continues with "no small stir among the soldiers," as well there might be, for a soldier paid for the escape of his prisoner with his own life. After this Herod departs for Caesarea. Josephus tells the story of the sudden death of Herod in Caesarea while he was there to attend the games held in honour of the emperor Claudius after being acclaimed as a god by his courtiers. His account shows how it is possible to write the same story from another point of view since the death shows no suggestion of a manifest divine intention; Agrippa simply dies an unexpected and unmourned death.

As Luke tells the story the acclamation came in the course of Herod's reception of inhabitants of Tyre and Sidon. These cities were not part of his kingdom, and the subject of contention between them is not clear. The way Josephus tells the story is helpful in showing how the events might have seemed to a historian who did not share Luke's perspective. For Luke, Herod has invited the fate that must befall the proud, heartless persecutor of God's people. He is struck down by the Lord's avenging angel and dies a death like the infamous Antiochus in Maccabean times (2 Macc 9:5-12).

THE RELIEF MISSION RETURNS TO ANTIOCH. 12:24-25.

> [24]But the word of God grew and multiplied.
>
> [25]And Barnabas and Saul returned from Jerusalem when they had fulfilled their mission, bringing with them John whose other name was Mark.

The minor summary re-iterates that persecution cannot impede the growth of the church. The whole episode is brought to a close with a note on the return of Barnabas and Saul to Antioch accompanied by John Mark. The question of the visits of Paul to Jerusalem is raised by v.25, which is best translated "Barnabas and Saul returned, having completed their mission in Jerusalem."

Luke has made it clear in this second part that he is not attempting a detailed picture of the origins of the earliest communities. He offers no account, for example, of the origin of the community Paul was received into at Damascus (9:19). Nor is he guided by chronological sequence; the stories about Philip, the conversion of Saul and Peter's baptism of the household of Cornelius interrupt the narrative of the Hellenist missioners expelled from Jerusalem (8:4; 11:19). It is likely that the church of Antioch was started before any ministry of either Peter or Paul to the pagans and that the Hellenists were those to first take that initiative.

Luke's picture is stylized. For him "the Twelve" or "the apostles" are established in Jerusalem, from which their mission starts and to which they reguarly return (8:25; 9:26), as guarantors of the continuity of the Church with the risen Christ not only in their "witness" and their "teaching" but in their supervision and approval of missionary initiatives as well. He has arranged the events of this section in this way to insist that the great work of the mission to the pagans was undertaken at the express invitation of God and with the sanction of the apostles and at the initiative of their leader.

The situation at the beginning of chapter 6 has changed significantly by the end of chapter 12. The initial persecution left "the apostles" in Jerusalem, but the persecution of chapter 12 had killed one of their number and forced the departure of Peter from Jerusalem. With his departure we find Peter and the apostles together only once more at the Council of Jerusalem. Jerusalem has lost its centrality. It no longer sends representatives to control the growth of the community. Paul goes "to visit the churches" entirely on his own initiative (15:36; 18:22; 19:21). Missionary activity radiates no longer from Jerusalem but from Antioch. The age of "the apostles" is over.

Part III

"To The Ends Of The Earth"

13:1 — 28:31

PART III

"TO THE ENDS OF THE EARTH"

SECTION 1.
MISSIONS OF PAUL AND BARNABAS.
13:1 - 15:35.

THE DISAPPEARANCE of Peter clears the stage for the great hero of the remainder of Acts. Chapters 13-14 describe the first missionary journey of Paul through Cyprus, the south coast of Asia Minor and into central Asia Minor, from Seleucia to Salamis to Paphos, thence to Perga in Pamphylia, through the towns of Lycaonia (Iconium, Lystra, Derbe) and the return through Lystra, Iconium, Antioch, Perga and the port of Attalia to Antioch. Not that the story begins as that of Paul. He appears as one of a group of leaders in the church of Antioch, commences the journey as junior partner to the veteran Barnabas and emerges suddenly as leader after a striking miracle at Cyprus.

The action begins in the mission-minded church of Antioch, Paul's centre in his future ventures, too (14:26; 18:22). As usual great events commence under the prompting of the Holy Spirit certainly, but with only that guidance necessary for the moment. God's intention is revealed in human reactions. Only after rejection in the synagogue, the logical commencement, does Paul declare God's will that he turn to the Gentiles. At other places in his story of Paul, Luke shows signs of relying on a kind of diary of his travels which provides some details of relatively insignificant daily detail. Though Luke's story of this first missionary journey can be compared with details of Paul's letters, the details of the journey remain vague and Paul's discourse at Antioch is similar in structure and themes, if not in all its elements, to missionary discourses we have already met. Luke's editorial hand is evident here in ways with which we have become familiar in earlier discourses; in transitions, connections between incidents and sections of the discourse, and in favourite Lucan themes that are emphasized. This first missionary journey is in many respects a summary of the whole missionary career of Paul; what happens here is typical of many later instances.

THE COMMISSION. "SET APART BARNABAS AND SAUL . . ." 13:1-3.

> **13** Now in the church at Antioch there were prophets and teachers, Barnabas, Symeon who was called Niger, Lucius of Cyrene, Manaen a member of the court of Herod the tetrarch, and Saul. [2]While they were worshipping the Lord and fasting, the Holy Spirit said, "Set apart for me Barnabas and Saul for the work to which I have called them." [3]Then after fasting and praying they laid their hands on them and sent them off.

The leaders of the Antioch community are a group of "prophets and teachers," functions sometimes distinguished in Paul's letters (cf. 1 Cor 14:26,29), though here probably applied indiscriminately to each of the group of five men. Barnabas heads the list, then Simeon who may be the Simeon mentioned again in 15:14, the otherwise unknown Lucius, then Manaen a boyhood companion of Herod Antipas, with Paul last. While they are at prayer the Holy Spirit speaks through a prophet, bringing together Barnabas and Saul for a task indicated in a very general way but already divinely decided. After a further period of prayer and fasting by way of preparation they are commended to God for their mission by the imposition of hands.

CYPRUS. "THE TEACHING OF THE LORD." 13:4-12.

> [4]So, being sent out by the Holy Spirit, they went down to Seleucia; and from there they sailed to Cyprus. [5]When they arrived at Salamis, they proclaimed the word of God in the synagogues of the Jews. And they had John to assist them. When they had gone through the whole island as far as Paphos, they came upon a certain magician, a Jewish false prophet, named Bar-Jesus. [7]He was with the proconsul, Sergius Paulus, a man of intelligence, who summoned Barnabas and Saul and sought to hear the word of God. [8]But Elymas the magician (for that is the meaning of his name) withstood them, seeking to turn away the proconsul from the faith. [9]But Saul, who is also called Paul, filled with the Holy Spirit, looked intently at him [10]and said, "You son of the devil, you enemy of all righteousness, full of all deceit and villainy, will you not stop making crooked the straight paths of the Lord? [11]And now, behold, the hand of the Lord is upon you, and you shall be blind and unable to see the sun for a time." Immediately mist and darkness fell upon him and he went about seeking people to lead him by the hand. [12]Then the proconsul believed, when he saw what had occurred, for he was astonished at the teaching of the Lord.

Situated on the sea lanes from Rome to Syria, Asia Minor and Greece, Cyprus was a strategic island prized also for its deposits of copper. It was Barnabas' home territory. There were Jews living there, and Barnabas and Saul preached "in the synagogues of the Jews." We hear nothing of their success or failure with the Jewish listeners; Barnabas and Saul, accompanied (the reader learns in an aside) by John Mark, proceed immediately to the other end of the island for Luke's main item of interest as far as Cyprus was concerned, the encounter between Saul and the Jewish magician Bar-Jesus. The Roman pro-consul Sergius Paulus is mentioned in inscriptions found in Cyprus and elsewhere, but his term of office cannot be dated.

The Roman official seeks out the company of Barnabas and Saul so that he can "hear the word of God." The magician (now called Elymas) opposes them. Paul, like Peter (cf. Acts 4:8) "full of the Holy Spirit" counters the magical arts of the man he declares to be "full of all deceit and villainy" and proclaims a blindness that strikes the magician and reduces him to the condition of "seeking people to lead him by the hand." Seeing the miracle and hearing the word bring about faith on the part of the pro-consul who is "astonished at the teaching of the Lord," confirmed as it is by a power vastly superior to that of the magician.

It is significant that Saul becomes Paul at the moment in Luke's story when the Spirit works so clearly through him and as he begins to move freely among Greeks and Romans. "Paul," the only name by which he calls himself in his letters, is a well-known Roman family name which he bore from birth. "Saul" was an added name used in Jewish circles. The change in name also corresponds to a change in status or role; from now on he acts as leader.

As with Philip in Samaria (8:13) so with Paul in Cyprus, "the word of the Lord" has subdued the mysterious and very real forces of magic. In some ways, too, the story is a counterpart to that of Peter and Simon Magus. Moreover, Luke has shown at the beginning of Paul's missionary career that an open-minded Roman official finds nothing in Christianity that is incompatible with his service of the empire.

ANTIOCH OF PISIDIA.
13:13-14.

> [13]Now Paul and his company set sail from Paphos, and came to Perga in Pamphylia. And John left them and returned to Jerusalem; [14]but they passed on from Perga and came to Antioch of Pisidia.

Luke gets Paul and Barnabas from Cyprus to Antioch of Pisidia within two verses, and these include a note about the totally unexplained return of John Mark to Jerusalem. He spares not a word to elaborate on the sea voyage from Cyprus, their reasons for leaving, or the very arduous journey through the mountains of central Asia Minor. The memory of Antiochus, the father of Seleucus, one of the generals of Alexander the Great was perpetuated in many Antiochs established in the era of the Seleucids. Antioch of Pisidia was, in fact, in Phyrgia near the border of Pisidia. It was the administrative centre of the southern part of the Roman province of Galatia, numbering many Jewish inhabitants.

The story depicts the typical pattern of Paul's missionary activity, beginning in the synagogue preaching to Jews and "God-fearing men" or Gentiles like Cornelius, rejection by the Jews, acceptance by the pagans, the birth of a new community, persecution arising out of the jealousy of the Jews, departure to another town and repetition of the cycle.

PAUL'S SPEECH.
"WHAT GOD PROMISED TO THE FATHERS."
13:14-43.

> And on the sabbath day they went into the synagogue and sat down. [15]After the reading of the law and the prophets, the rulers of the synagogue sent to them, saying, "Brethren, if you have any word of exhortation for the people, say it." [16]So Paul stood up, and motioning with his hands said:
>
> "Men of Israel, and you that fear God, listen. [17]The God of this people Israel chose our fathers and made the people great during their stay in the land of Egypt, and with uplifted arm he led them out of it. [18]And for about forty years he bore with them in the wilderness. [19]And when he had destroyed seven nations in the land of Canaan, he gave them their land as an inheritance, for about four hundred and fifty years. [20]And after that he

gave them judges until Samuel the prophet. [21]Then they asked for a king; and God gave them Saul the son of Kish, a man of the tribe of Benjamin, for forty years. [22]And when he had removed him, he raised up David to be their king; of whom he testified and said, 'I have found in David the son of Jesse a man after my heart, who will do all my will.' [23]Of this man's posterity God has brought to Israel a Saviour, Jesus, as he promised. [24]Before his coming John had preached a baptism of repentance to all the people of Israel. [25]And as John was finishing his course, he said, 'What do you suppose that I am? I am not he. No, but after me one is coming, the sandals of whose feet I am not worthy to untie.'

[26]"Brethren, sons of the family of Abraham, and those among you that fear God, to us has been sent the message of this salvation. [27]For those who live in Jerusalem and their rulers, because they did not recognise him nor understand the utterances of the prophets which are read every sabbath, fulfilled these by condemning him. [28]Though they could charge him with nothing deserving death, yet they asked Pilate to have him killed. [29]And when they had fulfilled all that was written of him, they took him down from the tree, and laid him in a tomb. [30]But God raised him from the dead; [31]and for many days he appeared to those who came up with him from Galilee to Jerusalem, who are now his witnesses to the people. [32]And we bring you the good news that what God promised to the fathers, [33]this he has fulfilled to us their children by raising Jesus; as also it is written in the second psalm,

'Thou art my Son,
today I have begotten thee.'

[34]And as for the fact that he raised him from the dead, no more to return to corruption, he spoke in this way,

'I will give you the holy and sure blessings of David.'

[35]Therefore he says also in another psalm,

'Thou wilt not let thy Holy One see corruption.'

> [36]For David, after he had served the counsel of God in his own generation, fell asleep, and was laid with his fathers, and saw corruption; [37]but he whom God raised up saw no corruption. [38]Let it be known to you therefore, brethren, that through this man forgiveness of sins is proclaimed to you, [39]and by him every one that believes is freed from everything from which you could not be freed by the law of Moses. [40]Beware, therefore, lest there come upon you what is said in the prophets:
> [41]'Behold, you scoffers, and wonder, and perish;
> for I do a deed in your days,
> a deed you will never believe, if one declares it to you.'"
>
> [42]As they went out, the people begged that these things might be told them the next sabbath. [43]And when the meeting of the synagogue broke up, many Jews and devout converts to Judaism followed Paul and Barnabas, who spoke to them and urged them to continue in the grace of God.

This first sample of Paul's missionary preaching is directed to a mixed audience of Jews and "God fearing" Gentiles in the Diaspora. Like Peter's major missionary discourses to Jews or "God-fearing men" it is a resumé of the history of salvation from God's choice of "the fathers" to the resurrection of Jesus, "Son" and "Saviour," the fulfilment for the children of "what God promised to the fathers" (v.32).

What is said of John the Baptist (vv.24-25) is characteristic of Luke, as are the terms used about the cross and resurrection (vv.27-31). He produces a discourse that is characteristically Pauline in its emphasis on the Risen Christ, author of justification (vv.38-39) and the content of God's promise (vv.32-33). The interpretation of Isaiah 55:3 and Psalm 16:10 (vv.34-37) is that of a Jewish Christian preacher formed in the rules of Jewish interpretation, and the use of the prophecy of Habakkuk (v.41) is likewise characteristic of Paul (cf. Rom 1:17).

Three addresses to the audience mark the three sections of the discourse which consists of a recitation of Israel's history (11:16-25), a summary of the career of Jesus with scriptural testimonies (vv.26-37) and a proclamation of forgiveness of sins coupled with a warning (vv.38-41).

The recitation of the history of Israel omits all reference to the patriarchal and Mosaic periods already amply treated by Stephen. Paul insists on what God has done for "this people of Israel" in His choice of them, care for them in Egypt, "bearing with them in the desert," giving them the land as their inheritance. He gave them judges and king Saul whom he "removed." Finally, He "raised up" David as king. The term is ambiguous; here it means the establishment of the Davidic line, but it prepares for the "raising up" of Jesus from the dead (v.30). The Jesus whom Paul is proclaiming is the "Saviour" God has "brought forth from the seed of David according to the promise." This discourse emphasizes the role of John the Baptist as the Gospel had done, his proclamation of a baptism of penance "for all the people Israel" and his express profession of the superiority of Jesus.

God's offer of this salvation comes in the message of the missioners (vv.26-37). Paul repeats the now familiar indictment against those responsible for the death of Jesus. He distinguishes "those who live in Jerusalem" and "their leaders" and offers the excuse of ignorance (v.17 cf. 3:17) at the same time as he insists on the innocence of Jesus. In this ignorance they were unconsciously fulfilling the prophecies they did not understand. At the climax of this section is the customary proclamation of the resurrection (v.30) and a reminder of the position of the apostles as "witnesses to the people." Paul does not rank himself and Barnabas with these witnesses. These two are not witnesses but "proclaimers of the Good News," offered to "us the children"; for what has happened in God's raising Jesus is the fulfilment of His promises to "the fathers."

What promises? Paul draws them from Psalm 2:7(v.33); Isaiah 55:3(v.34), and Psalm 16:10(v.35) already used in

Acts 2:25-28. Jesus is the Messianic King, enthroned by God as His Son by his resurrection and victory over death. Isaiah voices God's promise to give the "holy and sure blessings of David" (literally, "the trustworthy holy things" or covenant blessings). That promise is fulfilled in God's giving "the holy one who did not see corruption," namely the Risen Christ.

The final appeal to conversion (vv.38-41) carries with it an ominous warning. The Resurrection of Jesus fulfils all God's promises to "this people Israel." Now the message of the preacher offers them the forgiveness of their sins, and in Pauline terms "justification from all the things of which you could not be justified by the Law of Moses." He invokes Habakkuk (1:5) to show the peril of non-belief on the part of "this people Israel" which will perish while it sees "a deed you will never believe." The remainder of Luke's story will amply illustrate both of these possibilities in the regular rejection of Paul's message by the Jews and God's "visitation of the Gentiles, to take out of them a people to his name" (15:14).

Both consequences are exemplified in the immediate sequel. The only immediate reaction Luke notes is favourable, an invitation to "speak these words" on the following sabbath and a group of members of the synagogue, Jews and converts to Judaism, who follow Paul and Barnabas. The two urge them "to continue in the grace of God," namely the Good News they have received.

THE RESULT. "BEHOLD, WE TURN TO THE GENTILES." 13:44-52.

> [44]The next sabbath almost the whole city gathered together to hear the word of God. [45]But when the Jews saw the multitudes, they were filled with jealousy, and contradicted what was spoken by Paul, and reviled him. [46]And Paul and Barnabas spoke out boldly, saying, "It was necessary that the word of God should be spoken first

> to you. Since you thrust it from you, and judge yourselves unworthy of eternal life, behold, we turn to the Gentiles. [47]For so the Lord has commanded us, saying,
> 'I have set you to be a light for the Gentiles,
> that you may bring salvation to the uttermost parts of the earth.'"
>
> [48]And when the Gentiles heard this, they were glad and glorified the word of God; and as many as were ordained to eternal life believed. [49]And the word of the Lord spread throughout all the region. [50]But the Jews incited the devout women of high standing and the leading men of the city, and stirred up persecution against Paul and Barnabas, and drove them out of their district. [51]But they shook off the dust from their feet against them, and went to Iconium. [52]And the disciples were filled with joy and with the Holy Spirit.

Antioch was a very large city. The reader recognises literary licence in the phrase "almost the whole city gathered together to hear the word of God" (v.44). With a similar generalisation he characterises Paul's opponents as "full of jealousy" (cf. 5:17; 7:9) in their "contradicting" (cf. Lk 2:34; 20:27; Acts 28:19) and "reviling" (cf. 18:6). These were typical responses Luke was familiar with from the half-century of missionary activity that preceded the writing of Acts. They were not the only responses Paul and others encountered from Jewish audiences as Luke's story shows (14:1; 17:10-12; 21:20).

This typical scene sets the pattern for subsequent episodes and points towards the final result of his missionary activity (cf. 28:26-28). Paul's words (vv.46-48) do not make Jewish unbelief the primary cause of the Gentile mission. Similar programmatic statements (2:39; 3:25-26) have already established the position of the Jews in the work of salvation. The refusal of many, however hard to understand, still falls into place in God's plan.

In justification of his move Paul uses the prophecy of Isaiah (49:6). Paul's missionary work fulfils God's words concerning the Suffering Servant. As "light for the nations" he will "bring salvation to the uttermost parts of the earth." The phrase shows that it is in Paul's missionary work (which occupies virtually the rest of the Acts) that the final phase of the commission of the risen Jesus to the apostles (1:8) will be fulfilled. The typical "Pauline missionary cycle" is completed by the birth of a community of Gentile believers, the spread of the word "throughout the region," persecution from the Jews and departure for another place, there to recommence the cycle. The advent of salvation brings rejoicing and praise of God (cf. 11:18; 21:20). Not all believe, only those who in God's design "were ordained to eternal life." By a ritual act of rejection (Lk 9:5; 10:11) the two fulfil the injunction of Jesus to missioners whose message is rebuffed, and then depart.

ICONIUM.
"A GREAT COMPANY BELIEVED, BOTH JEWS AND GREEKS."
14:1-7.

> **14** Now at Iconium they entered together into the Jewish synagogue, and so spoke that a great company believed, both of Jews and of Greeks. [2]But the unbelieving Jews stirred up the Gentiles and poisoned their minds against the brethren. [3]So they remained for a long time, speaking boldly for the Lord, who bore witness to the word of his grace, granting signs and wonders to be done by their hands. [4]But the people of the city were divided; some sided with the Jews, and some with the apostles. [5]When an attempt was made by both Gentiles and Jews, with their rulers, to molest them and to stone them, [6]they learned of it and fled to Lystra and Derbe, cities of Lycaonia, and to the surrounding country; [7]and there they preached the gospel.

Iconium was within the same Roman province of Galatia about 90 miles away. The initial venture in the synagogue is crowned with success among its Jewish and proselyte members. Active rejection follows from Jews who influence the pagans against Paul and Barnabas. They remain courageous, "relying on the Lord." The "signs and wonders" that He "continually gave through their hands" are the testimony He himself bears to "the word of his grace."

So far Luke has been careful to reserve the title "apostles" to the Twelve. The only exceptions to this usage appear in 14:4,14 in which the title is extended to Paul and Barnabas. The fact that Paul's mission has just been proclaimed as completing the commission of the risen Lord to the apostles (1:8) and that practically identical terms are used of them as of "the apostles" (14:3 cf. 5:12) makes it likely that Luke has not been forgetful in this detail and that he has systematically attempted to establish Paul's equality in this stage of the mission with the Twelve. In a similar fashion the term "witness" which has been used to describe the privileged position of the Twelve will gradually be applied to Paul (22:15; 26:16).

The townsfolk are divided into two very clear groups. On the one side stand "the apostles"; on the other the adversaries of their mission, "the Jews." Paul and Barnabas escape from an attempt which is in the offing "to molest them and to stone them" by fleeing eastward into the cities of Lycaonia with their ethnically distinct population.

LYSTRA.
14:8-20.

> [8]Now at Lystra there was a man sitting, who could not use his feet; he was a cripple from birth, who had never walked. [9]He listened to Paul speaking; and Paul, looking intently at him and seeing that he had faith to be made well, [10]said in a loud voice, "Stand upright on your feet." And he sprang up and walked. [11]And when the crowds saw what Paul had done, they lifted up their voices, saying in Lycaonian, "The gods have come down

to us in the likeness of men!" [12]Barnabas they called Zeus, and Paul, because he was the chief speaker, they called Hermes. [13]And the priest of Zeus, whose temple was in front of the city, brought oxen and garlands to the gates and wanted to offer sacrifice with the people. [14]But when the apostles Barnabas and Paul heard of it, they tore their garments and rushed out among the multitude, crying, [15]"Men, why are you doing this? We also are men, of like nature with you, and bring you good news, that you should turn from these vain things to a living God who made the heaven and the earth and the sea and all that is in them. [16]In past generations he allowed all the nations to walk in their own ways; [17]yet he did not leave himself without witness, for he did good and gave you from heaven rains and fruitful seasons, satisfying your hearts with food and gladness." [18]With these words they scarcely restrained the people from offering sacrifice to them.

[19]But Jews came there from Antioch and Iconium; and having persuaded the people, they stoned Paul and dragged him out of the city, supposing that he was dead. [20]But when the disciples gathered about him, he rose up and entered the city; and on the next day he went on with Barnabas to Derbe.

For the story of the mission in Lystra Luke has organised materials of different origin into a relatively coherent whole. A miracle story (vv.8-10), a narrative passage (vv.11-14), a short discourse (vv.15-17) and concluding brief narrative (vv.18-20) have been brought together. The result is a picture of the impact of the powerful message of the missioners on the religion of the pagans and the briefest outline possible of a missionary discourse, together with an example of the rejection and suffering that typically rounded off the "missionary cycle."

The response of the Lycaonian crowd far exceeds the miracle that evoked it. Wonder-workers were not unknown in their world and even a cure as remarkable as this was hardly likely to produce a spontaneous and universally acclaimed identification of the wonder worker with their gods, least of all by the local priest of Zeus. It can also be asked just what kind of things Paul has been saying to a pagan crowd before the miracle if only his discourse after it can dissuade them from the kind of idolatry they propose. On the other hand it is likely that Luke was familiar with a Hellenistic legend originating in those parts about a visit of Zeus and Hermes to Phrygia, and that he uses it to describe the reaction of the pagans to the power of the bearers of the Good News. It is not, then, factual information based on the reminiscences of Paul and Barnabas that he is providing; he is using a known Hellenistic literary motif as literary embellishment for a story about the first encounter of the Good News with a wholly pagan environment.

The story of the cure of the man crippled from birth (vv.8-10) is similar enough in some details to the story of Peter's cure of the lame man (3:2-5) to be taken as an instance of Luke's "equalisation process," establishing Paul as a counterpart to Peter and stamping on each the likeness of Jesus. It also differs in many respects and in one significant detail in particular. The cripple has been listening to Paul speaking, and Paul's message has already touched him. Paul sees that he has "faith to be healed," or, in more literal translation, "to be saved." The message brings faith and faith brings salvation.

Paul has been speaking in Greek and has been understood by the cripple. In the narrative (vv.11-14) the crowds cry out in their own dialect, hence Paul has no suspicion of what they plan to do. The wonder has convinced them that the father of the gods, no less than Zeus himself, has come among them with his spokesman Hermes, this latter being Paul. The official representative of pagan religion, the priest of Zeus, brings oxen for sacrifice and garlands for such honoured guests. Only now, after all the hubbub proceeding apace, but in a dialect they do not understand, are "the apostles" alerted to the meaning of the furore. They are about to be offered divine honours! There follows a very effective non-verbal communication of their horror transparent enough to break the language barrier, and their rejection of this deification.

Brief as they are, Paul's words at Lystra (vv.15-17) are the first missionary discourse to a completely pagan audience that Luke offers. Paul is a long way from the Jerusalem audiences of Peter, even from those proselytes or "God-fearing" pagans attached to a synagogue. Standing in front of a pagan temple he outlines a number of the themes that will be orchestrated in the discourse in Athens (17:22-31), some of them already articulated by Jewish missioners in times prior to Christ in their polemic against idol worship and familiar to us from Paul's writings (cf. 1 Thess 1:9-10).

The narrative has established the missioners as far superior to the wonder workers or "divine men" of the Hellenistic world; even official pagan religion is prepared to offer them divine honours! However exalted their mission and their powers, they remain men. The Good News they bring is precisely to call men from these "vain things" (cf. Jer 2:5) to the one God who, by contrast with deaf, dumb and dead idols, is "the living God," who alone made all things, an Israelite faith professes (cf. Ex 20:11). In past generations God let the Gentiles go their own way, but even so His kindly providence that extended to them bore witness to Him. As for present times—now that God has revealed Himself to the pagans through the apostolic message—we hear nothing at this point.

The pendulum swings very quickly indeed from near-defication to near-death (vv.18-20). Jews from Iconium persuade a very volatile crowd, who had been restrained not long before with difficulty from offering divine honours to the missioners, to stone Paul. The fate he had escaped in Iconium is visited on him in Lystra. Almost laconically, and with no suggestion of miraculous aid, Luke has Paul who, after being stoned, had been dragged outside the city to be left for dead, simply stand up and start the "missionary cycle" all over again. Suffering, persecution, even stoning, are part of the missioner's lot, but they are incapable of impeding the mission.

RETURN TO ANTIOCH. "A DOOR OF FAITH FOR THE GENTILES." 14:21-28.

> [21]When they had preached the gospel to that city and had made many disciples, they returned to Lystra and to Iconium and to Antioch, [22]strengthening the souls of the disciples, exhorting them to continue in the faith, and saying that through many tribulations we must enter the kingdom of God. [23]And when they had appointed elders for them in every church, with prayer and fasting, they committed them to the Lord in whom they believed.
>
> [24]Then they passed through Pisidia, and came to Pamphylia. [25]And when they had spoken the word in Perga, they went down to Attalia; [26]and from there they sailed to Antioch, where they had been commended to the grace of God for the work which they had fulfilled. [27]And when they arrived, they gathered the church together and declared all that God had done with them, and how he had opened a door of faith to the Gentiles. [28]And they remained no little time with the disciples.

The concluding section of the first missionary journey shows in a series of typical activities Paul's dealings with communities already established. Paul and Barnabas "strengthen the souls of the disciples," they "encourage them" to perseverance in the faith in the face of persecution, and they establish church order by "appointing elders in every church."

Finally they return to the church which commissioned them to proclaim God's great deeds. The church of Antioch echoes to a refrain like that heard in Jerusalem after Peter initiated the admission of the pagans (11:18).

FROM ANTIOCH TO JERUSALEM. "UNLESS YOU ARE CIRCUMCISED." 15:1-5.

> **15** But some men came down from Judea and were teaching the brethren, "Unless you are circumcised according to the custom of Moses, you cannot be saved." [2]And when Paul and Barnabas had no small dissension and debate with them, Paul and Barnabas and some of the others were appointed to go up to Jerusalem to the apostles and the elders about this question. [3]So, being sent on their way by the church, they passed through both Phoenicia and Samaria, reporting the conversion of the Gentiles, and they gave great joy to all the brethren. [4]When they came to Jerusalem, they were welcomed by the church and the apostles and the elders, and they declared all that God had done with them. [5]But some believers who belonged to the party of the Pharisees rose up, and said, "It is necessary to circumcise them, and to charge them to keep the law of Moses."

With chapter 15 Luke has reached the heart of his second volume. The first stages of the missionary programme outlined in the command of the Risen Lord (1:8) have been sketched in the story of the Jerusalem community and in the missionary ventures of Philip in Samaria and Judaea. The story of the conversion of Cornelius' household by Peter, the establishment of the "ecumenical" church of Antioch, and the success of the mission of Paul and Barnabas lead directly to the decisions taken in Jerusalem.

Luke's account begins with a dispute in Antioch which is referred to the church of Jerusalem and resolved in a process in which apostles and elders, Paul and Barnabas, Peter and James and the whole community reach a unanimous decision under the guidance of the Holy Spirit that removes the last of the obstacles to the spread of the witness to "the ends of the earth." It is the last act of Peter and the "apostles." From now on the story will focus uniquely on Paul and the Gentile churches and the movement that will take Paul to Rome.

The main lines of Luke's canvas are orderly and clear. In Antioch men from Jerusalem deny the validity of the Gentile mission in insisting on the necessity of the law of Moses. A delegation from Antioch carries the dispute to the Church in Jerusalem. The unanimous decision resolves the dispute in favour of the Gentiles and establishes their freedom from the Law of Moses. Some minimal demands are made on them and the decisions are transmitted to the church in Antioch by a delegation from the church in Jerusalem. The number of participants in the action is surprising. In Antioch the community share in a decision to send "Paul, Barnabas and some others" (v.2). News of the conversion of the Gentiles delights "all the brothers" in the churches of Phoenicia and Samaria (v.3). In Jerusalem they are welcomed by "the church and the apostles and elders" (v.4). The objections of "some of the party of the Pharisees" (v.5) are met by "the apostles and elders" (v.6). "All the assembly" (v.12) listen to Peter and James, Barnabas and Paul. "The Apostles and elders and the whole Church" send Judas and Silas (v.22) to Antioch, where "the congregation" receives the letter and Judas and Silas encourage "the brothers."

The Jerusalem meeting is a model of concord. James endorses Peter's experience at Caesarea as indication of God's will for the Gentiles (v.14). "The apostles and elders" accept the decision taken by James and send a letter embodying the decision to the Gentiles in Antioch, Syria and Cilicia (v.23). It is the Holy Spirit who creates this unanimity, which extends to the testimony of the prophet Amos (v.15), and approves the stand of Paul and Barnabas.

How much of this picture is Luke's own creation? It is generally admitted that he has connected items previously separated by transitional verses of his own composition such as vv.1-2, 22-23. But there is very wide divergence in the assessments of scholars of the contribution of Luke, for example, in the speeches of Peter and James and the letter sent by the apostles and elders. A similar divergence of views applies to the question of the relationship of Luke's story of this journey of Paul to Jerusalem and the autobiographical details provided by Paul in Gal 2:1-10. Paul mentions no regulations imposed on him at his meeting with the "pillars" of the Jerusalem church, James, Cephas and John at the meeting in which they approved his Gospel and his mission to the Gentiles. Paul's rebuke to Peter at Antioch (Gal 2:11-21) makes it clear that neither he nor Peter knew anything at that time of the provisions enjoined by the Jerusalem letter which would have settled the issue, and his answer to questions from Corinth concerning use of meat sacrificed to idols (1 Cor 8-10) similarly shows no knowledge of the prohibition of meat sacrificed to idols.

Faced by these and similar difficulties many scholars conclude that in his reconstruction Luke draws on two historical recollections only, one of a meeting at which Jerusalem leaders agreed that Gentiles could be admitted to the community without being obliged to circumcision, the other the long standing custom obtaining in mixed communities of Jews and Gentiles that required of Gentile Christians the observance of certain Jewish cultic regulations for the sake of fellowship with Jewish Christian members of the community. The hypothesis adopted here is as follows: Luke makes a composite portrait of what were two separate meetings. The first was that recorded by Paul in Gal 2:1-10, a meeting in which the Jerusalem authorities showed their agreement with the principle of Gentile freedom from the Law. The second meeting took place later when Paul was not present. This meeting dealt with the precise issue of relations between Jewish and Gentile Christians in mixed communities in Antioch, Syria and Cilicia, and resolved that the same kinds of demands be made on Gentile Christians in those circumstances as were made of foreigners resident in Israel.

In the present story in Acts the controversy originates with the arrival of a party from Jerusalem insisting on the necessity of circumcision for salvation. The point at issue is the observance of the Law of Moses; there is no question of the specific laws to be mentioned in v.29. The question touches the heart of the community's life as well as of the missionary methods of the Antioch church, exemplified in the missionary journey of Paul and Barnabas in chapters 13-14. Because of the turbulent debate between the Jerusalem party and Paul and Barnabas the community decides to send a delegation to "the apostles and elders," the authorities of the Jerusalem community. (In Gal 2:2 Paul says his visit was motivated by a "revelation").

They journey by way of Phoenicia and Samaria. In 11:19 Luke has touched on the evangelization of Phoenicia. Phoenicia and Samaria are differentiated from "the pagans." They are obviously regarded as comparable to Jewish Christian communities, but the news of "the conversion of the pagans" brings them "great joy." Arrived in Jerusalem the delegation is warmly received by "the church and the apostles and the elders," and again Paul and Barnabas warm to the theme we are becoming accustomed to, "the great things God has done" (cf. Acts 14:27) in the success of the Gentile mission. However the question that had caused their journey from Antioch is raised again, very explicitly, by a specific group of converted Pharisees.

PETER'S SPEECH.
15:6-11.

> [6]The apostles and the elders were gathered together to consider this matter. [7]And after there had been much debate, Peter rose and said to them, "Brethren, you know that in the early days God made choice among you, that by my mouth the Gentiles should hear the word of the gospel and believe. [8]And God who knows the heart bore witness to them, giving them the Holy Spirit just as he did to us; [9]and he made no distinction between us and them, but cleansed their hearts by faith. [10]Now therefore why do you make trial of God by putting a yoke

upon the neck of the disciples which neither our fathers nor we have been able to bear? [11]But we believe that we shall be saved through the grace of the Lord Jesus, just as they will."

"The apostles and elders" are convoked. "After much debate" Peter offers his testimony. This discourse (as also that of James to follow) is neither missionary nor apologetic but ecclesial, comparable to 1:16-20 addressed to the community itself at a crucial turning point on a matter decisive for its life and action. Peter reminds the audience that the conversion of the Gentiles commenced with his own activity in the house of Cornelius. The matter was decided by God "ages ago." The "reader of hearts" (cf. 1:24) knows the inner worthiness of persons and has borne witness to his choice of the Gentiles by giving them the gift of the Holy Spirit. Nor can they be regarded as in any way impure, for God has "cleansed their hearts by faith." If God, then, has signified his acceptance of Gentiles who do not observe the Law, then it would be to defy his manifest will to attempt to subject to the Law people who have not observed the law but are already "disciples." (The language of v.10 is that of Luke's time and community; no faithful Jew saw the law of Moses as an intolerable yoke). Similarly the terms of v.11 have a very Pauline ring (cf. 13:38-39; Gal 5:6; 6:15). Luke thus shows Peter's accord with the underlying principles of the Gentile mission of Paul.

JAMES' SPEECH.
15:12-21.

[12]And all the assembly kept silence; and they listened to Barnabas and Paul as they related what signs and wonders God had done through them among the Gentiles. [13]After they finished speaking, James replied, "Brethren, listen to me. [14]Symeon has related how God first visited the Gentiles, to take out of them a people for his name. And

with this the words of the prophets agree, as it is written,
[16]'After this I will return,
and I will rebuild the dwelling of David, which has fallen;
I will rebuild its ruins,
and I will set it up,
[17]that the rest of men may seek the Lord,
and all the Gentiles who are called by my name,
[18]says the Lord, who has made these things known from of old.'
[19]Therefore my judgment is that we should not trouble those of the Gentiles who turn to God, [20]but should write to them to abstain from the pollutions of idols and from unchastity and from what is strangled and from blood. [21]For from early generations Moses has had in every city those who preach him, for he is read every sabbath in the synagogues."

In Luke's story Barnabas and Paul are practically sandwiched between Peter and James; it is understandable that Paul's version differs significantly in accent and emphasis. The "whole assembly" listens to their familiar refrain "what signs and wonders God has done through them among the Gentiles."

The speech of James is Luke's construction. The decision he states is taken from the letter that follows (vv.28,29) and his scriptural justification is very unlikely from a Jewish Christian. The speech formulates the principle of the vocation of the Gentiles, then draws some practical conclusions which are justified by an appeal to the Law (v.21).

James is in full accord with Peter that in the conversion of the household of Cornelius "God visited the Gentiles to take out of them a people for his name." The phrase is Scriptural in style and vocabulary. Deuteronomy calls Israel "a people holy to the Lord . . . a people for his own possession out of all the peoples that are on the face of the earth"

(Deut 14:2; 26:18), and Zechariah prophesied that in the eschatological era "many nations shall join themselves to the Lord and shall be "my people" (Zech 2:11). That day has come; the pagan converts have joined faithful Israel in the finally constituted Chosen People.

Not only is James in accord with Peter in this interpretation, but the Scriptures are also in accord with them both. James cites Amos 9:11-12 as a proof. In the Hebrew Bible the prophecy refers to the return of Israel from Exile; the ruins of David's city will be rebuilt and the Davidic dynasty restored. The ancient pagan enemies Edom, Moab, Philistia will be subjugated. But where the Hebrew text reads "that they may possess the remnant of Edom and all the nations that are called by my name," the Greek version translates "that the rest of men may seek the Lord and all the gentiles who are called by name." It thus makes a prophecy of the conversion of the pagans out of a prophecy of Israel's conquest of the pagans. James' argument depends on those points precisely at which the Greek translation differs from the Hebrew text. This is hardly likely as a historical recollection of an address by a Jewish Christian speaker addressing a Jewish Christian audience in Jerusalem.

In view of this purpose of God to join Gentiles to Jews in the Chosen People, James decides that convert Gentiles should not be submitted to the Law and circumcision. It seems surprising that in the next breath he formulates a series of demands on Gentile Christians. The practises proscribed are among those which Israelite law forbade for resident aliens (Lev 17-18) so that Israelites could associate freely with them without ritual contamination. The Gentiles are to refrain from meat sacrificed to idols, marriage within forbidden degrees of consanguinity and affinity, from meat not ritually slaughtered and with blood still in it. These are ritual, not moral prescriptions, and they meet the most basic sensitivities of Jewish Christians in their association with Gentile Christians in worship and daily life.

THE APOSTOLIC LETTER. 15:22-29.

> [22]Then it seemed good to the apostles and the elders, with the whole church, to choose men from among them and send them to Antioch with Paul and Barnabas. They sent Judas called Barsabbas, and Silas, leading men among the brethren, [23]with the following letter: "The brethren, both the apostles and the elders, to the brethren who are of the Gentiles in Antioch and Syria and Cilicia, greeting. [24]Since we have heard that some persons from us have troubled you with words, unsettling your minds, although we gave them no instructions, [25]it has seemed good to us in assembly to choose men and send them to you with our beloved Barnabas and Paul, [26]men who have risked their lives for the sake of our Lord Jesus Christ. [27]We have therefore sent Judas and Silas, who themselves will tell you the same things by word of mouth. [28]For it has seemed good to the Holy Spirit and to us to lay upon you no greater burden than these necessary things: [29]that you abstain from what has been sacrificed to idols and from blood and from what is strangled and from unchastity. If you keep yourselves from these, you will do well. Farewell."

The whole assembly "apostles and elders with the whole Church" choose a delegation of two to send to Antioch with Paul and Barnabas, the otherwise unknown Judas called Barsabbas and Silas who is to become Paul's missionary co-worker. The delegates are entrusted with a letter to the Gentile churches in Antioch and the Roman provinces of Syria and Cilicia. No mention has so far been made of missionary activity in these latter two areas though Acts 15:41 assumes already established communities there.

The letter disowns the trouble makers as unrepresentative of the attitude of the Jerusalem church, praises Paul and Barnabas, introduces the delegates and communicates the decision. It underlines the unanimity and concord of the community (v.25) and ascribes the decision to the Holy Spirit (v.28). The decision already stated in v.20 is repeated in a slightly differing formulation.

FROM JERUSALEM TO ANTIOCH. 15:30-35.

> [30]So when they were sent off, they went down to Antioch; and having gathered the congregation together, they delivered the letter. [31]And when they read it, they rejoiced at the exhortation. [32]And Judas and Silas, who were themselves prophets, exhorted the brethren with many words and strengthened them. [33]And after they had spent some time, they were sent off in peace by the brethren to those who had sent them. [35]But Paul and Barnabas remained in Antioch, teaching and preaching the word of the Lord, with many others also.

In a few lines Luke returns the action to the point at which it has started. The return of the party with the letter brings comfort and joy to the previously disturbed community. The prophetic activity of Judas and Silas encourages them and strengthens their faith, while Paul, Barnabas and others continue their ministry as teachers and evangelists.

SECTION 2.
MISSIONS OF PAUL.
15:36 - 21:14.

Now that he has shown how the major issues affecting the mission reached a successful resolution in the "Council" of Jerusalem, Luke is free to make of Paul the central figure of the second half of his book. Peter has made his exit, Barnabas disappears to Cyprus, and the last mention of "the apostles" at Jerusalem occurs very early in this section. Luke chooses Paul as the figure who can best illustrate the spread of the Good News. The commission that was given to "the apostles" will now be carried on by Paul.

The division between first and second missionary journeys is more for convenience than because Luke has emphatically divided them. The story begins with Paul's very general intention of visiting communities already established in the first missionary journey. It is not Paul, however, but the Holy Spirit who is responsible and who directs the missioners into the heart of the Greek world in his own wonderful way. The Good News is offered regularly to the Jews first; it is usually their refusal which motivates the preaching to the Gentiles who receive it warmly.

The second journey takes Paul to communities which we know from his own letters as well as from Luke. The epistles to the Thessalonians, Philippians, and Corinthians offer us a more detailed picture of their domestic composition and problems than does Luke. They provide a very helpful corrective to impressions one might get from reading Luke's narrative alone. Comparison of the letters with the Acts helps particularly to clarify Luke's intention in insisting on the elements he chooses and shows that his main interest is in the foundation of these well-known centres and in illustrating the paradoxical divine guidance which turns seeming disaster into missionary milestones.

The accounts of the second and third journeys differ from that of the first in the often detailed nature of Luke's information and in the appearance of the "We Sections" which raise the question of Luke's participation in the events or the availability of a travel diary of a companion of Paul. Not all the material is of this kind, however; some passages are very bare digests. At times Luke elaborates a story of divine help with the customary devices of his world, at others his information is limited or faulty.

The pro-consulate of Gallio offers one firm point in establishing the chronology of this period. An inscription found at Delphi concerning Gallio makes it clear that he commenced his term before August 52. His one year term probably ran from May or June of A.D. 51 till A.D. 52.

PAUL AND BARNABAS. "THERE AROSE A SHARP CONTENTION." 15:36-41.

> [36]And after some days Paul said to Barnabas, "Come, let us return and visit the brethren in every city where we proclaimed the word of the Lord, and see how they are." [37]And Barnabas wanted to take with them John called Mark. [38]But Paul thought best not to take with them one who had withdrawn from them in Pamphylia, and had not gone with them to the work. [39]And there arose a sharp contention, so that they separated from each other; Barnabas took Mark with him and sailed away to Cyprus, [40]but Paul chose Silas and departed, being commended by the brethren to the grace of the Lord. [41]And he went through Syria and Cilicia, strengthening the churches.

As Luke describes it the great missionary venture commences with an initiative of Paul, a generous proposal by Barnabas, a vigorous argument leading to their separation and the constitution of not one, but two mission bands. Not long after their return from Jerusalem Paul suggests a return to the communities founded in the first missionary journey. Barnabas, the man who had gained entry into a very suspicious Jerusalem community for the converted persecutor (9:27), brought Paul to Antioch from Tarsus (11:25), and probably started as leader in the first missionary journey (cf. 13:2,7), wants to take John Mark along. John Mark appears suddenly on the scene; he has last been heard of in Jerusalem (13:13). Despite the success of Barnabas in "discerning the Spirit" in Paul's own case, Paul insists on the primacy of the "work" of the mission and will not tolerate "one who had withdrawn from them in Pamphylia and not gone with them to the work." It is a case of irreconcilable conflict. Barnabas sails off with John Mark to his home land and into literary oblivion; he appears no more in Acts. The story of the rest of the book is the story of Paul, who chooses Silas, the representative of the Jerusalem community (15:22,27,32) and thus guarantees Paul's acceptance by the mother community on the mission to the pagans. After an official leave-taking they commence their journey.

Paul's own account of an irreconcilable difference with Barnabas can be found in Gal 2:11-14, the story of Peter's withdrawal from the company of Gentile Christians in Antioch because of the arrival of Jewish Christians from Jerusalem. Paul claimed that "even Barnabas was carried away by their hypocrisy" and Barnabas shared in the vigorous rebuke Paul delivered to Peter. This makes it difficult to accept Luke's story as being based on clear historical recollections at least as to its details, but however the origin of Luke's story is to be explained, it is invaluable as a recognition of the human realities of the early Church, a suggestion of the human differences and clashes of temperament and judgment that Luke makes no attempt to hide because, far from disrupting the spread of the Good News, they become in God's purpose the seedbed of new developments.

DERBE AND LYSTRA. "THE CHURCHES WERE STRENGTHENED IN THE FAITH." 16:1-5.

16 And he came also to Derbe and to Lystra. A disciple was there named Timothy, the son of a Jewish woman who was a believer; but his father was a Greek. [2]He was well spoken of by the brethren at Lystra and Iconium. [3]Paul wanted Timothy to accompany him; and he took him and circumcised him because of the Jews that were in those places, for they all knew that his father was a Greek. [4]As they went on their way through the cities, they delivered to them for observance the decisions which had been reached by the apostles and elders who were at Jerusalem. [5]So the churches were strengthened in the faith, and they increased in numbers daily.

Paul returns to the churches he had founded (14:6,8) and finds in these young churches a man fitted to help in the work of the mission. Timothy is the son of a Jewish mother and Gentile father, a union forbidden by the Law (Deut 7:3). He has not been reared as a Jew, he is as yet uncircumcised. Paul has Timothy circumcised "because of the Jews that were in those places," to avoid obstacles to the mission in synagogue preaching. This is difficult to understand in view of Paul's own statements of his attitude to the liberty of the Gentiles from circumcision and the Law (cf. Gal 5:2-3), and the decision at Jerusalem (15:5-11). It may, perhaps, be understood as an example of his practise as outlined in 1 Cor 9:20. To the churches in these regions Paul communicates the decisions which had been reached by "the apostles and elders who were at Jerusalem." This could have been, in point of historic fact, the decision freeing Gentile Christians from the observance of the Law, but Luke's composition of chapter 15 gives the impression that the other restrictions were transmitted to these churches, too, though they had been dictated only to the churches of Antioch, Syria and Cilicia. The last mention of "the apostles" underlines the fact that the transfer of the Lord's initial injunction from the first group in Jerusalem is complete. From now on the mission of the Church, for Luke, is in the hands of Paul and his companions as they reach out to the Gentile world. The section concludes with a conventional Lucan summary insisting on growth (cf. 2:41, 47 etc.) and deepened faith (cf. Col 2:5; 1 Pet 5:9).

PAUL'S VISION. "GOD HAD CALLED US TO PREACH THE GOSPEL TO THEM." 16:6-10.

> [6]And they went through the region of Phrygia and Galatia, having been forbidden by the Holy Spirit to speak the word in Asia. [7]And when they had come opposite Mysia, they attempted to go into Bithynia, but the Spirit of Jesus did not allow them; [8]so, passing by Mysia, they went down to Troas. [9]And a vision appeared to Paul in the night: a man of Macedonia was standing beseeching him and saying, "Come over to Macedonia and help us." [10]And when he had seen the vision, immediately we sought to go on into Macedonia, concluding that God had called us to preach the gospel to them.

Man proposes; God disposes. Paul had proposed a visit to the communities he had previously founded, but the spread of the Good News depends on God. In ways Luke makes no attempt to explain, Paul's plans are changed. The party travels through Phrygia and the Galatian region. Ancient Phrygia straddled what later became the Roman provinces of Galatia and Asia. Mysia was the northwest region of the Roman province of Asia.

The geographical details show a westerly progress to Troas, the port near the site of ancient Troy. How far north in the province of Galatia the journey took them is problematical. Twice their plans are checked by "the Holy Spirit" who is "the Spirit of Jesus," preventing them from turning south to cities on the coast of Asia Minor such as Ephesus or north to the cities on the Black Sea. At Troas the direction of the mission is communicated to Paul by divine intervention in a vision as it has been communicated to Peter (10:3,17,19; 11:5). In verse 10 the first of the "We Sections" commences with the departure for Macedonia.

PHILIPPI.
16:11-40.

[11]Setting sail therefore from Troas, we made a direct voyage to Samothrace, and the following day to Neapolis, [12]and from there to Philippi, which is the leading city of the district of Macedonia, and a Roman colony. We remained in this city some days; [13]and on the sabbath day we went outside the gate to the riverside, where we supposed there was a place of prayer; and we sat down and spoke to the women who had come together. [14]One who heard us was a woman named Lydia, from the city of Thyatira, a seller of purple goods, who was a worshipper of God. The Lord opened her heart to give heed to what was said by Paul. [15]And when she was baptized, with her household, she besought us, saying, "If you have judged me to be faithful to the Lord, come to my house and stay." And she prevailed upon us.

[16]As we were going to the place of prayer, we were met by a slave girl who had a spirit of divination and brought her owners much gain by soothsaying. [17]She followed Paul and us, crying, "These men are servants of the Most High God, who proclaim to you the way of salvation." [18]And this she did for many days. But Paul was annoyed, and turned and said to the spirit, "I charge

you in the name of Jesus Christ to come out of her." And it came out that very hour.

[19]But when her owners saw that their hope of gain was gone, they seized Paul and Silas and dragged them into the market place before the rulers; [20]and when they had brought them to the magistrates they said, "These men are Jews and they are disturbing our city. [21]They advocate customs which it is not lawful for us Romans to accept or practice." [22]The crowd joined in attacking them; and the magistrates tore the garments off them and gave orders to beat them with rods. [23]And when they had inflicted many blows upon them, they threw them into prison, charging the jailer to keep them safely. [24]Having received this charge, he put them into the inner prison and fastened their feet in the stocks.

[25]But about midnight Paul and Silas were praying and singing hymns to God, and the prisoners were listening to them, [26]and suddenly there was a great earthquake, so that the foundations of the prison were shaken; and immediately all the doors were opened and every one's fetters were unfastened. [27]When the jailer woke and saw that the prison doors were open, he drew his sword and was about to kill himself, supposing that the prisoners had escaped. [28]But Paul cried with a loud voice, "Do not harm yourself, for we are all here." [29]And he called for lights and rushed in, and trembling with fear he fell down before Paul and Silas, [30]and brought them out and said, "Men, what must I do to be saved?" [31]And they said, "Believe in the Lord Jesus, and you will be saved, you and your household." [32]And they spoke the word of the Lord to him and to all that were in his house. [33]And he took them the same hour of the night, and washed their wounds, and he was baptized at once, with all his family. [34]Then he brought them up into his house, and set food before them; and he rejoiced with all his household that he had believed in God.

[35]But when it was day, the magistrates sent the police, saying, "Let those men go." [36]And the jailer reported the

> words to Paul, saying, "The magistrates have sent to let you go; now therefore come out and go in peace." [37]But Paul said to them, "They have beaten us publicly, uncondemned, men who are Roman citizens, and have thrown us into prison; and do they now cast us out secretly? No! let them come themselves and take us out." [38]The police reported these words to the magistrates, and they were afraid when they heard that they were Roman citizens; [39]so they came and apologised to them. And they took them out and asked them to leave the city. [40]So they went out of the prison, and visited Lydia; and when they had seen the brethren, they exhorted them and departed.

The secton concerning Paul's arrival at Philippi and his stay there is woven of different kinds of literary materials, including a section of travel narrative (vv.11-12), the story of an exorcism (vv.16-18), a miracle story of the freeing of Paul and Silas from their bonds and the conversion of their jailer (vv.25-34), and a narrative of their expulsion from the city (vv.35-40).

Paul recalled the "suffering and shameful treatment" he encountered in Philippi (1 Thess 2:2). His special affection and indebtedness to this community is also a matter of record (Phil 4:14). At several points his letter permits us to check Luke's story of the foundation of these churches.

A quick journey of two days leaves the travellers at Neapolis, nowadays Kavalla, the port of Philippi. The Roman province of Macedonia was divided into four districts. Philippi, though not a capital city, was a prominent town in the first of these districts. On the sabbath they commence preaching to a small Jewish congregation, not in a synagogue, but at a "place of prayer" by a river, possibly the Gangites, a mile and a quarter from the city. God "opens the heart" of the wealthy Lydia, enabling her to hear as he enables Paul to speak. She and her household are baptized; her generous hospitality provides Paul with a base of operations.

Paul's mission is acknowledged by an unexpected source and the power of the Gospel again triumphs over the power of magic (cf. 13:10-12). In a story reminiscent of the encounters of Jesus with men possessed by unclean spirits who recognise the secret of his identity and mission (cf. Mk 1:24; Lk 4:34,41; 8:28) Paul exorcises a slave girl, whose powers of divination were a source of profit to her owners. The spirit is overcome by the invocation of "the name of Jesus Christ."

The accusation formulated against Paul and Silas before the magistrate (the Roman duumviri who exercised jurisdiction in Roman colonial cities) goes far beyond anything in their activities that the narrative has so far suggested. This is the first time Paul comes into contact with the Roman judicial system. The charge of disturbing the peace is one which will regularly be laid against him, though in fact it is the people who follow and harass him who are regularly inciting the crowds (cf. 17:6 etc.), but nothing in Luke's account justifies the charge of "advocating customs unlawful for Romans" of which they are accused. Luke makes it clear that from first to last in his encounters with Roman law nothing has been found in the conduct of Paul which could be construed as contrary to Roman law.

The miracle story (vv.25-34) that follows illustrates God's wonderful response to the prayers of his persecuted servants. Paul and Silas, bound in the deepest recesses of the prison, praise God in their chains. God responds with an earthquake of a most wonderful kind, opening all the doors, freeing them from their bonds. The frantic jailer is about to commit suicide without even so much as investigating, when he is restrained by the voice of Paul. The man then offers the model response to God's manifest approval of his messengers; he asks the central question in the life of every religious man and Paul provides the Christian answer in his proclamation of salvation through belief in Christ. The jailer and all his household (suddenly transferred to the prison) listen to "the word of the Lord"; then all repair to the jailer's house where all are baptized, the wounds of the missioners are tended and hospitality offered. Luke closes the story with a characteristic touch emphasizing the joy that salvation brings to the man's house.

A number of features of this story are customary in pagan as well as Christian sources of wonderful interventions. The collection of inconsistencies shows that Luke is emphasizing in ways congenial to the story tellers of his time how God responds to the prayer of his helpless servants, to turn their distress into an occasion for the salvation of others. Imprisonment and chains cannot impede the spread of the Good News.

The story of Paul's stay in Philippi is concluded in a more sober, if ironic, narrative in which the injustice of the proceedings is brought out (vv.35-40). The law forbade Roman citizens to be flogged. A pair of fearful and humbled magistrates are obliged to escort the men they had summarily beaten and imprisoned in a kind of solemn procession out of the town.

THESSALONICA.
17:1-9.

> **17** Now when they had passed through Amphipolis and Apollonia, they came to Thessalonica, where there was a synagogue of the Jews. [2]And Paul went in, as was his custom, and for three weeks he argued with them from the scriptures, [3]explaining and proving that it was necessary for the Christ to suffer and to rise from the dead, and saying, "This Jesus, whom I proclaim to you, is the Christ." [4]And some of them were persuaded, and joined Paul and Silas; as did a great many of the devout Greeks and not a few of the leading women. [5]But the Jews were jealous, and taking some wicked fellows of the rabble, they gathered a crowd, set the city in an uproar, and attacked the house of Jason, seeking to bring them out to the people. [6]And when they could not find them, they dragged Jason and some of the brethren before the city authorities, crying, "These men who have turned the world upside down have come here also, [7]and Jason has received them; and they are all acting against the decrees

> of Caesar, saying that there is another king, Jesus." [8]And the people and the city authorities were disturbed when they heard this. [9]And when they had taken security from Jason and the rest, they let them go.

The next stage in the journey is through Macedonia along the great Via Egnatia which ran from Philippi in the north to the Adriatic. Thessalonica was the capital of the second district of Macedonia about ninety-five miles from Philippi and a major seaport then as it is now.

Luke underlines Paul's beginning in the synagogue as his customary procedure. His first volume has provided, in the practise of Jesus, the precedent for this procedure (Lk 4:16). The commission of the Risen Lord to the apostles (Lk 24:45-46) is carried on by Paul as he "opens the Scriptures" and "proves it was necessary for the Christ to suffer and rise from the dead," thus leading up to the proclamation that "this Jesus, whom I proclaim to you, is the Christ."

The pattern of successful preaching, jealousy of the Jews, persecution and withdrawal already set in the first missionary journey, is repeated. Some Jews and many of the God-fearing Gentiles attach themselves to Paul and Silas. As adherents of the synagogue are taken from them the jealousy of the Jews is aroused and they provoke a "popular demonstration" against the trouble makers. The resulting persecution culminates in a trial on the charge of breaking the peace linked with the charge, potentially enormously more dangerous, of sedition in "saying that there is another king, Jesus." The issue is resolved by placing Paul's host on a bond.

BEROEA.
"THEY RECEIVED THE LORD WITH ALL EAGERNESS."
17:10-15.

> [10]The brethren immediately sent Paul and Silas away by night to Beroea; and when they arrived they went

into the Jewish synagogue. [11]Now these Jews were more noble than those in Thessalonica, for they received the word with all eagerness, examining the scriptures daily to see if these things were so. [12]Many of them therefore believed, with not a few Greek women of high standing as well as men. [13]But when the Jews of Thessalonica learned that the word of God was proclaimed by Paul at Beroea also, they came there too, stirring up and inciting the crowds. [14]Then the brethren immediately sent Paul off on his way to the sea, but Silas and Timothy remained there. [15]Those who conducted Paul brought him as far as Athens; and receiving a command for Silas and Timothy to come to him as soon as possible, they departed.

Beroea was fifty miles to the south, away from the Via Egnatia and other main roads. Here, by contrast to Thessalonica, the members of the synagogue offer a model reception to the message of Paul and Silas. The community that originates is largely Jewish, though Luke likes to note the adherence of "not a few Greek women of high standing as well as men." The inevitable trouble is not locally instigated but initiated by Jews from Thessalonica. In 1 Thess 3:1-2 Paul writes that Timothy accompanied him to Athens and returned to Thessalonica. Luke's statement in v.14 is either abridged or inaccurate.

PAUL AT ATHENS. "HIS SPIRIT WAS PROVOKED WITHIN HIM." 17:16-21.

[16]Now while Paul was waiting for them at Athens, his spirit was provoked within him as he saw that the city was full of idols. [17]So he argued in the synagogue with the Jews and the devout persons, and in the market place every day with those who chanced to be there. [18]Some also of the Epicurean and Stoic philosophers met him. And some said, "What would this babbler say?" Others

> said, "He seems to be a preacher of foreign divinities"—because he preached Jesus and the resurrection. [19]And they took hold of him and brought him to the Areopagus, saying, "May we know what this new teaching is which you present? [20]For you bring some strange things to our ears; we wish to know therefore what these things mean." [21]Now all the Athenians and the foreigners who lived there spent their time in nothing except telling or hearing something new.

The golden age of Athens lay five centuries before Paul. On his arrival in 50 A.D. it was not even the capital of the Roman province of Achaia. It has been eclipsed by new Roman colonies, especially by the provincial capital Corinth. Even though it had become "the museum of classical culture for the Greek world" it stands for Luke as a symbol of the religion and philosophy of the pagan Hellenistic world. Paul's arrival is a highlight in the mission to the pagans.

The centre of the city was the rocky hill of the Acropolis. The Agora or market place was at its base and the Areopagus, a very rocky and much lower hill, was to the east. Here the ancient Athenian tribunal had met, and though later it sat in the market place, the name Areopagus stayed with the tribunal.

The two principal and rival schools of philosophy were the Epicureans and the Stoics. Epicurus (342-271 B.C.) gave his name to a school of pragmatists for whom the wise conduct of human life was to be attained by reliance on the evidence of the senses and the elimination of superstition and belief in supernatural intervention. Plain living and virtue would lead to perfect harmony of body and mind. The Stoics were founded by Zeno of Citium (320 B.C.). They regarded the world as an organic ordered whole animated and directed by intelligence, with an active principle, God, and a passive principle, matter. For them the true end of human activity was life in harmony with nature, mankind a universal brotherhood, freedom attainable by detachment and independence from the outer world.

The introductory narrative (vv. 16-21) shows Paul in this pagan world, disturbed by its idol worship, debating not only with Jews in the synagogue but with Stoic and Epicureans in the Agora. Their curiosity is piqued. The epithet "this parrot" (v. 18), a phrase used of birds that pick up grain no matter where they find it and then of "seekers of the second rate at second hand." More ominously his message sounds like "a new teaching concerning alien gods," as if Anastasis (the resurrection) was the female consort of the god Jesus. This was the charge that had led to the death of Socrates. Paul is led to the Areopagus (either the council or the place) for what, though dangerous, is yet an informal discussion.

PAUL'S SPEECH: "IN EVERY WAY YOU ARE VERY RELIGIOUS." 17:22-34.

> [22]So Paul, standing in the middle of the Areopagus, said: "Men of Athens, I perceive that in every way you are very religious. [23]For as I passed along, and observed the objects of your worship, I found also an altar with this inscription. 'To an unknown god.' What therefore you worship as unknown, this I proclaim to you. [24]The God who made the world and everything in it, being Lord of heaven and earth, does not live in shrines made by man, [25]nor is he served by human hands, as though he needed anything, since he himself gives to all men life and breath and everything. [26]And he made from one every nation of men to live on all the face of the earth, having determined allotted periods and the boundaries of their habitation, [27]that they should seek God, in the hope that they might feel after him and find him. Yet he is not far from each one of us, [28] for

'In him we live and move and have our being';
as even some of your poets have said,
'For we are indeed his offspring.'
[29]Being then God's offspring, we ought not to think that the Deity is like gold, or silver, or stone, a representation by the art and imagination of man. [30]The times of ignorance God overlooked, but now he commands all men everywhere to repent, [31]because he has fixed a day on which he will judge the world in righteousness by a man whom he has appointed, and of this he has given assurance to all men by raising him from the dead."

[32]Now when they heard of the resurrection of the dead, some mocked; but others said, "We will hear you again about this." [33]So Paul went out from among them. [34]But some men joined him and believed, among them Dionysius the Areopagite and a woman named Damaris and others with them.

The discourse (vv.22-31) is the first extended sample of a missionary discourse to a pagan audience. Some if its themes Luke has already stated in the telegrammatic discourse of Paul at Lystra (14:15-17). It is clearly a summary and it is equally a composition of Luke concerning the God who has remained unknown to the pagans and who finally reveals himself to them in the message of the apostle. Neither Luke nor Paul were the first to attempt to convert the Hellenistic world to monotheism. Jewish thinkers and apologists had developed over several centuries their own manners and approach to the proclamation of the one God to the pagans. The Old Testament provides instances of satirical polemic against idolatry (Wis 13-15; Is 40-42); less well-documented is another approach in which Jewish missioners showed that the Jewish faith offered the fulfilment of the noblest aspirations of pagan philosophers and poets. It is this latter approach that this discourse adopts.

The introduction (vv.22-23) and conclusion (vv.30-31) can easily be distinguished. The body of the discourse consists of one long sentence (vv.24-27) which is separated from the inference Paul wishes to draw from it (v.29) by a quotation from the poets (v.28).

Paul's diplomatic beginning praises the manifest devoutness of the Athenians which shows not only in the multiplicity of their objects of worship but especially in the altar "to an unknown god." Ancient Greek writers talk of altars to "unknown gods," certainly, but no such altar inscription has yet been discovered. This God, Paul claims, as yet unknown but nonetheless worshipped in Athens, is the God he announces. He thus avoids the charge that had led Socrates to death and moves into the body of his monotheistic discourse.

What kind of God is He and what is His purpose for men? As Jewish monotheism asserts He is maker of the world and Lord of the universe (cf. Is 42:5), not enclosed within the world process like the supreme being of the Stoics. Hence he does not live in man-made temples, pagan or Jewish (cf. 7:48). Paul used an idea familiar to the Greeks when he asserts that God needs nothing since it is he who preserves everything in life. He is in action in the realms of nature and history. It is He who had made the entire race of men from one man, who has guided the course of each nation's history, assigns the epochs of their rise and fall (cf. Dan 2:21), marks out their borders (cf. Job 12:23; Deut 32:8).

The purpose of this providential guidance is that they should "seek Him." Whether they will find Him or not is uncertain; men fumble towards a problematical outcome despite the fact that God is so close. Two allusions to Greek poets serve as proof of this assertion. "In him we live and move and are" echoes words of Epimenedes of Cnossos of the sixth century which had a perfectly acceptable pantheistic meaning to pagans but also expresses the belief of Jews and Christians in man's absolute dependence on the one God. The second quotation is from Aratus, a third century poet; and while it expresses the Stoic belief in the unity of men, it also states Luke's belief in the origin of all men from God.

The conclusion is clear and hardly surprising to Paul's sophisticated audience since it roundly condemned what they would have regarded as the superstitions of popular pagan religion. Granted man's relationship of dependence on God no artifact contrived by man can represent God. Paul's concluding appeal, however, passes abruptly from what might have seemed commonplace to a call for a change of heart arising out of God's final intervention in human history which has started a new era in His relations with humanity. So far God has left unpunished the ignorance which they have admitted (v.20). But "now," with the offer of true knowledge in the preaching of the apostle, that era is past. They must repent. God has fixed a time of judgment, established a judge, and accredited him "to all men everywhere" by raising him from the dead.

The cultured Hellenistic audience dissolves at the mention of the resurrection of the dead, a concept totally unacceptable to both Stoics and Epicureans. Some mock openly, some laconically suggest an adjournment sine die, some few come to belief.

By comparison with Paul's own teaching on the ignorance of the pagans in Rom 1:21-32, this speech passes a different judgment on the philosophy and religion of the pagans. Paul writes of the widespread immorality of the pagans as God's punishment for their refusal to worship Him despite clear signs of his "eternal power and deity" in the created world. In Luke's discourse Paul claims that God has "overlooked the times of ignorance" in the past and concedes that the pagans have indeed been worshipping the true God even though they did not know Him. Luke has Paul point to the aspirations of the Greek poets as proof just as he drew on the words of the Prophets before Jewish audiences. Greek wisdom can be a preparation for the Gospel; purged of its errors it is capable of stating the message of the one true God.

This was the situation of missioners in Luke's time. The Gospel was being proclaimed to pagans with little or no connection with the synagogue. The proclamation of the one true God was drawing on those elements in Greek philosophy and poetry that served at least as hints of what the true God was. But for Greeks as well as Jews the real stumbling block was faith in the Risen Christ.

CORINTH. "DO NOT BE AFRAID . . . SPEAK!" 18:1-17.

18 After this he left Athens and went to Corinth. [2]And he found a Jew named Aquila, a native of Pontus, lately come from Italy with his wife Priscilla, because Claudius had commanded all the Jews to leave Rome. And he went to see them; [3]and because he was of the same trade he stayed with them, and they worked, for by trade they were tentmakers. [4]And he argued in the synagogue every sabbath, and persuaded Jews and Greeks.

[5]When Silas and Timothy arrived from Macedonia, Paul was occupied with preaching, testifying to the Jews that the Christ was Jesus. [6]And when they opposed and reviled him, he shook out his garments and said to them, "Your blood be upon your heads! I am innocent. From now on I will go to the Gentiles." [7]And he left there and went to the house of a man named Titius Justus, a worshipper of God; his house was next door to the synagogue. [8]Crispus, the ruler of the synagogue, believed in the Lord, together with all his household; and many of the Corinthians hearing Paul believed and were baptized. [9]And the Lord said to Paul one night in a vision, "Do not be afraid, but speak and do not be silent; [10]for I am with you, and no man shall attack you to harm you; for I have many people in this city." [11]And he stayed a year and six months, teaching the word of God among them.

> [12]But when Gallio was proconsul of Achaia, the Jews made a united attack upon Paul and brought him before the tribunal, [13]saying, "This man is persuading men to worship God contrary to the law." [14]But when Paul was about to open his mouth, Gallio said to the Jews, "If it were a matter of wrongdoing or vicious crime, I should have reason to bear with you, O Jews; [15]but since it is a matter of questions about words and names and your own law, see to it yourselves; I refuse to be a judge of these things." [16]And he drove them from the tribunal. [17]And they all seized Sosthenes, the ruler of the synagogue, and beat him in front of the tribunal. But Gallio paid no attention to this.

Corinth was the capital of the Roman province of Achaia, the "emporium of the Empire," with its two ports, the Lechaion opening on to the Adriatic and Cenchreae on to the Aegean. Paul's own correspondence provides an extensive view of the situation of this mercurial community some time after its foundation and provides invaluable insights into the circumstances of his arrival (1 Cor 2:1-5). Luke's seventeen verses are the merest summary of as many months, pointing to the significant and characteristic moments in its development.

On arrival Paul takes up lodgings with two Jewish Christians, Aquila and his wife Priscilla. The faith did not arrive in Corinth with Paul. They had been expelled from Rome in A.D. 49 by Claudius' edict aimed at putting an end to constant disturbances between Jews and Christians. The story begins quietly with Paul working at his trade, during the week probably that of leatherworker, and arguing in the synagogue on the sabbath. With the arrival of Timothy and Silas (cf. 17:15; 1 Thess 3:2) he is enabled to devote himself full time to preaching, almost certainly because they brought with them substantial financial support (cf. 2 Cor 11:8). As in Antioch of Pisidia (13:46,50) it is opposition from within the synagogue that leads to a complete break. The gesture of shaking the dust from his clothes (cf. 13:51) signifies complete separation; the phrase "your blood be upon your heads" (v.6) lays the responsibility for the situation on the guilty parties (cf. Ez 18:13; Lev 20:9). Paul goes to live with a Gentile previously attached to the synagogue, Titius Justus, and begins the new phase in his teaching in premises cheek by jowl with the synagogue. The conversion of the synagogue leader Crispus is a high point (v.8); his conversion commences a stream of converts. It can only be a matter of time, past experience shows, before open conflict will break out.

But before further trials Paul is strengthened by God. Paul has a vision of his Lord by night. The terms are reminiscent of Gen 26:24 and Is 43:5. He may be persecuted but God's protection will be with his work since the Lord has a great "people" in Corinth (cf. 15:14). The vision explains Paul's long stay in Corinth as expressly due to the guidance of Christ and it prepares us for the next dangerous episode.

Gallio was brother of the philosopher Seneca. With the change in the Roman administration the Jews try to bring Paul to trial on the charge of "persuading men to worship God contrary to the law." The charge would have been very dangerous if Paul's activities had been judged as promoting a religion prohibited by Roman law. The whole future of the mission would have been compromised. What is important to Luke is the attitude of the Roman official who disregards the charge and sees the episode as factional infighting between Jews, as a matter not of Roman but of Jewish law. He finds no reason to condemn Paul for "wrongdoing or vicious crime," refuses to interfere in matters of Jewish law, disperses the crowd and pays no attention to them even as they turn violently on their unsuccessful leader.

FROM CORINTH TO ANTIOCH. "I WILL RETURN TO YOU IF GOD WILLS." 18:18-23.

> [18]After this Paul stayed many days longer, and then took leave of the brethren and sailed for Syria, and with

him Priscilla and Aquila. At Cenchreae he cut his hair, for he had a vow. [19]And they came to Ephesus, and he left them there; but he himself went into the synagogue and argued with the Jews. [20]When they asked him to stay for a longer period, he declined; [21]but on taking leave of them he said, "I will return to you if God wills," and he set sail from Ephesus.

[22]When he landed at Caesarea, he went up and greeted the church, and then went down to Antioch. [23]After spending some time there he departed and went from place to place through the region of Galatia and Phrygia, strengthening all the disciples.

Neither from Athens nor from Corinth does Paul depart hurriedly or as a fugitive. He leaves a well established community before his return to Antioch. Priscilla and Aquila accompany him, settle in Ephesus, and become actively engaged in the work of the mission there (18:19,26). Luke depicts Paul at this point as a devout Jew who takes a Nazirite vow before commencing a journey which will take him to Jerusalem. This detail causes difficulties since according to Num 6:1-21 the shaving of the head comes at the completion of the period of the vow and is to be done in the Temple. Luke is not recording something of which he was a witness or about which he had clear information (cf. 21:23). Paul's brief visit to Ephesus and his preaching in the synagogue is an anticipation of his longer stay on his third missionary journey. What community Paul greeted (v.22) is uncertain, though Luke seems to mean that Paul visited the community in Jerusalem.

APOLLOS.
"HE ONLY KNEW THE BAPTISM OF JOHN."
18:24-28.

[24]Now a Jew named Apollos, a native of Alexandria, came to Ephesus. He was an eloquent man, well versed in

> the scriptures. [25]He had been instructed in the way of the Lord; and being fervent in spirit, he spoke and taught accurately the things concerning Jesus, though he knew only the baptism of John. [26]He began to speak boldly in the synagogue; but when Priscilla and Aquila heard him, they took him and expounded to him the way of God more accurately. [27]And when he wished to cross to Achaia, the brethren encouraged him, and wrote to the disciples to receive him. When he arrived, he greatly helped those who through grace had believed, [28]for he powerfully confuted the Jews in public, showing by the scriptures that the Christ was Jesus.

A period of about two years intervened before Paul lived up to his promise to return to Ephesus (18:21). The administrative centre of the Roman province of Asia was an ideal centre for missionary operations. The city was the hub of one of the most thickly populated areas in Asia Minor, a region of over five hundred towns and cities. The seaport was an important commercial centre, linked by sea with Rome and the granaries of the Empire in Syria and Egypt, and by the overland trade routes with Persia and India. More important in Luke's picture was its magnificent temple of Artemis which was one of the seven wonders of the world and which placed it along with Athens and Jerusalem as one of the three "holy cities." Centre of a widespread cult of the goddess of fertility, it was likewise famous for its magic charms, usually inscribed in leaflets or little scrolls and books of incantations known as "Ephesian Writings."

Luke knew that Paul did not found the Christian community in Ephesus, but that the city had been a major centre of Paul's apostolic activity. From Ephesus his emissaries founded the churches of Colossae, Laodicaea and Hierapolis in the Lycus valley (Col 4:13), and from Ephesus he wrote the epistle to the Galatians, the letters to the Corinthians and possibly the epistle to the Philippians.

It is from these letters that we are enabled to supplement the account of Luke and check his picture against elements of Paul's own autobiography to establish the particular vantage point Luke adopts and what interests his presentation is calculated to serve. In this section Luke shows Paul encountering the Jewish religion in the synagogue, pagan religion in its magical practises and one of its major shrines, and also sectarian groups closely related to Christianity. This suggests that Luke had a wider acquaintance with a range of preachers, teachers and sectaries than the examples he offers.

Luke makes no claim to be an eye-witness of the events he narrates. The "We-Section" (16:10-17) stops at Philippi and does not take up again till Troas (20:5). Two sections (18:24-28; 19:13-20) do not involve Paul himself. Such evidence as unresolved inconsistencies in the details of stories like that of Apollos and the disciples of John the Baptist (19:1-7), the generalising summary about Paul's miraculous powers (19:11-12), signs of folklore and the exuberance of the story teller, characteristically Lucan phrases such as the summary of 19:20 alert us to the fact that he is tailoring his sources and shaping then to communicate his distinctive message.

Verses 24-28 interrupt the journey of Paul and seem almost an interlude. Together with the following story (19:1-7) this episode suggests something of the diversity of teachers proclaiming the Christian message and religious groups related to the Christian community in Ephesus. The story supposes a Jewish Christian community in good standing with the synagogue. Apollos is a Jewish Christian from Alexandria. He is eloquent and shares many of the same gifts as Paul. He is capable of reading the Christian meaning in the Old Testament Scriptures and is instructed in "the way of the Lord" (where or by whom Luke does not say). Fervent or "aglow with the Spirit" (cf. Rom 12:11), he "speaks and teaches accurately the things about Jesus" and "speaks out boldly in the synagogue." Only vv.25c-26 suggest any flaw in what is otherwise a picture of a Spirit-endowed preacher - but what a flaw! Apollos knows "only the baptism of John." Despite this there is no mention of his being baptized; he is simply given "more accurate instruction in the way of God" by Priscilla and Aquila, Paul's co-workers, then given letters of recommendation to the Christians of Achaia where his gifts greatly assist the communities in apologetics against the Jews.

Paul's own letters show a guarded attitude towards Apollos (1 Cor 1:12; 3:4-11,22; 4:6; 16:12) and to the very gifts Luke ascribes to him (cf. 1 Cor 2:1-5). Luke's story, not without inconsistency, subordinates Apollos to Paul by having Paul's co-workers complete this imperfect instruction and incorporate him into the mission which, in Luke's perspective, was originally confided to "the apostles" and is now continued authoritatively by Paul.

DISCIPLES OF THE BAPTIST. "BAPTIZED IN THE NAME OF THE LORD JESUS." 19:1-7.

> **19** While Apollos was at Corinth, Paul passed through the upper country and came to Ephesus. There he found some disciples. [2]And he said to them, "Did you receive the Holy Spirit when you believed?" And they said, "No, we have never even heard that there is a Holy Spirit." [3]And he said, "Into what then were you baptized?" They said, "Into John's baptism." [4]And Paul said, "John baptized with the baptism of repentance, telling the people to believe in the one who was to come after him, that is, Jesus." [5]On hearing this, they were baptized in the name of the Lord Jesus. [6]And when Paul had laid his hands upon them, the Holy Spirit came on them; and they spoke with tongues and prophesied. [7]There were about twelve of them in all.

A similar inconsistency marks the connected story of a group Paul encounters on his arrival in Ephesus. Luke calls them "disciples," that is "Christians." Paul's question prompts the admission that not only have they not received the Holy Spirit but that they "have never even heard that there is a Holy Spirit," an impossible statement on the part of Jews and equally impossible on the part of anybody closely connected with the community led by people like Aquila and Priscilla. This group Paul both instructs and baptizes.

The instruction elaborates on the relationship between John and Jesus, a relationship very carefully marked out by Luke in his first volume and already spelled out briefly in 13:24-25. It makes sense only for those who need very basic instruction on Jesus as the one in whom the Baptist called the people of God to believe. They are baptized "in the name of the Lord Jesus," and the apostle imposes hands on them. What follows is another "Pentecost." In Ephesus, as previously in Caesarea and Jerusalem, the gift of the Spirit is manifested in prophecy and ecstatic speech. The apostle has brought about a complete integration of followers of the Baptist into the Christian community. Verse 7 suggests, perhaps, that this is another group of leaders, an Ephesian "twelve" comparable to the Hellenist "seven" (cf. 6:5).

PAUL AND THE SYNAGOGUE. "HE WITHDREW FROM THEM." 19:8-10.

> [8]And he entered the synagogue and for three months spoke boldly, arguing and pleading about the kingdom of God; [9]but when some were stubborn and disbelieved, speaking evil of the Way before the congregation, he withdrew from them, taking the disciples with him, and argued daily in the hall of Tyrannus. [10]This continued for two years, so that all the residents of Asia heard the word of the Lord, both Jews and Greeks.

So far a largely Jewish-Christian community has co-existed peacefully with the synagogue. In Luke's stock phrases Paul "speaks out boldly," "argues" and "seeks" to persuade" his Jewish audience about the coming of the Kingdom of God. The reader awaits the almost inevitable rejection (cf. 13:45; 14:2; 17:5) which precipitates Paul's withdrawal to establish a base for his daily ministry in the lecture hall of Tyrannus. Luke concludes with the generalizing summary (v.10) emphasizing the spread of the word.

THE POWER OF PAUL. "GOD DID EXTRAORDINARY MIRACLES." 19:11-20.

> [11]And God did extraordinary miracles by the hands of Paul, [12]so that handkerchiefs or aprons were carried away from his body to the sick, and diseases left them and the evil spirits came out of them. [13]Then some of the itinerant Jewish exorcists undertook to pronounce the name of the Lord Jesus over those who had evil spirits, saying, "I adjure you by the Jesus whom Paul preaches." [14]Seven sons of a Jewish high priest named Sceva were doing this. [15]But the evil spirit answered them, "Jesus I know and Paul I know; but who are you?" [16]And the man in whom the evil spirit was leaped on them, mastered all of them, and overpowered them, so that they fled out of that house naked and wounded. [17]And this became known to all residents of Ephesus, both Jews and Greeks; and fear fell upon them all; and the name of the Lord Jesus was extolled. [18]Many also of those who were now believers came, confessing and divulging their practices. [19]And a number of those who practised magic arts brought their books together and burned them in the sight of all; and they counted the value of them and found it came to fifty thousand pieces of silver. [20]So the word of the Lord grew and prevailed mightily.

Luke first illustrates the impact of the Gospel on this pagan environment in a summary (vv.11-12) concerning Paul's miraculous powers of healing, which is followed by the story of the Jewish exorcists (vv.13-17) and its sequel in the public burning of books of magical spells (vv.18-20).

The summary shows the same king of healing power that emanated from Jesus (Lk 6:19; 8:44) and Peter (Acts 5:12-15) now at work in Paul both for the healing of illnesses and the expulsion of evil spirits.

The power of "the name of the Lord Jesus" by virtue of which Paul achieves these wonders is illustrated in another way in the story of the Jewish exorcists. The story bears signs of folklore. Sceva is a Roman name. No Jewish high-priest of that name is known, and it is very unlikely that the Jewish high-priest lived in Ephesus. There is admirable irony in a situation in which Paul's ascendancy is so great that seven exorcists of a very influential Jewish family aid the apostle in an attempt to exorcise one man. They carefully invoke the name that seems to be the secret of Paul's power only to learn very painfully that "the name of the Lord Jesus" is no magic incantation but an utterance of Christian faith.

The immediate consequence is the final break of Ephesian Christians with their pagan past. They confess their magical practices as sinful and the victory of the Gospel over the power of magic is completed in a public burning of the widely esteemed "Ephesian Writings." Verse 20 is a summary parallel to those of 6:7; 12:24 showing "the word of the Lord" as a personified force.

PAUL'S PLANS FOR THE FUTURE. "I MUST ALSO SEE ROME." 19:21-22.

[21]Now after these events Paul resolved in the Spirit to pass through Macedonia and Achaia and go to Jerusalem, saying, "After I have been there, I must also see

> Rome." [22]And having sent into Macedonia two of his helpers, Timothy and Erastus, he himself stayed in Asia for a while.

This note about Paul's plans for the future is inserted prior to the grand finale of his stay in Ephesus. What Paul proposes is, in fact, an outline of the rest of Acts. For Luke the "must" Paul states lies far deeper than the project of an individual missionary; the plan he enunciates is God's. The divine "must" that governed the life of Jesus (e.g. Lk 2:49; 17:25) and was outlined in the Scriptures (Lk 22:37) extends to the spread of the message of salvation "to the ends of the earth" (cf. Acts 23:11). Luke shows in advance that Paul's departure is not forced by the riot to follow; it is already decided by Paul and is one more step in accomplishing what lies in God's design.

RIOT.
"THERE AROSE NO LITTLE STIR CONCERNING THE WAY."
19:23-41.

> [23]About that time there arose no little stir concerning the Way. [24]For a man named Demetrius, a silversmith, who made silver shrines of Artemis, brought no little business to the craftsmen. [25]These he gathered together, with the workmen of like occupation, and said, "Men, you know that from this business we have our wealth. [26]And you see and hear that not only at Ephesus but almost throughout all Asia this Paul has persuaded and turned away a considerable company of people, saying that gods made with hands are not gods. [27]And there is danger not only that this trade of ours may come into disrepute but also that the temple of the great goddess Artemis may count for nothing, and that she may even be deposed from her magnificence, she whom all Asia and the world worship."

> [28]When they heard this they were enraged, and cried out, "Great is Artemis of the Ephesians!" [29]So the city was filled with the confusion; and they rushed together into the theatre, dragging with them Gaius and Aristarchus, Macedonians who were Paul's companions in travel. [30]Paul wished to go in among the crowd, but the disciples would not let him; [31]some of the Asiarchs also, who were friends of his, sent to him and begged him not to venture into the theatre. [32]Now some cried one thing, some another; for the assembly was in confusion, and most of them did not know why they had come together. [33]Some of the crowd prompted Alexander, whom the Jews had put forward. And Alexander motioned with his hand, wishing to make a defence to the people. [34]But when they recognised that he was a Jew, for about two hours they all with one voice cried out, "Great is Artemis of the Ephesians!" [35]And when the town clerk had quieted the crowd, he said, "Men of Ephesus, what man is there who does not know that the city of the Ephesians is temple keeper of the great Artemis, and of the sacred stone that fell from the sky? [36]Seeing then that these things cannot be contradicted, you ought to be quiet and do nothing rash. [37]For you have brought these men here who are neither sacrilegious nor blasphemers of our goddess. [38]If therefore Demetrius and the craftsmen with him have a complaint against any one, the courts are open, and there are proconsuls; let them bring charges against one another. [39]But if you seek anything further, it shall be settled in the regular assembly. [40]For we are in danger of being charged with rioting today, there being no cause that we can give to justify this commotion." [41]And when he had said this, he dismissed the assembly.

Luke has shown the impact of Paul and his message on the magical practises for which Ephesus was renowned; the concluding episode of his stay (vv.24-41) shows their impact on the world-wide worship of Artemis and the fame of her temple. The lively and at times confusing narrative is punctuated by two speeches in which Luke's message is heard most clearly. The silversmith Demetrius calls a meeting of his guild whose prosperity is being undermined by Paul. So far no silver models of the shrine of Artemis have been found, though silver images of Artemis and terra cotta images of the temple of the mother goddess and patroness of fertility have been. The speech of Demetrius (vv.24-27) is a testimonial to the power of Paul and the spread of his message condemning idol worship not only "in Ephesus, but throughout all Asia." His appeal is nicely calculated to sanctify the profit motive by the invocation of religious feeling and local loyalties. The enraged artisans throw the city into confusion by their repeated chant of the ceremonial acclamation of the goddess.

The action in the theatre (vv.29-34) is difficult to follow. Paul's companions Gaius and Aristarchus are dragged there as if for trial or even lynching. Alexander is introduced in what seems an effort by the Jews to dissociate themselves from Paul, but the Jewish advocate is shouted down before he can utter a word. Paul wishes to make a personal appearance at what, after all, is a meeting supposedly concerned with his activities, but is restrained by the Asiarchs, the most influential citizens in the province of Asia, elected annually as civil and probably pagan religious functionaries. No more is heard of Demetrius.

The speech of the town clerk (vv.35-40) calms the assembly. As argument v.35 is hardly very cogent, it simply denies the claim of Demetrius (v.28) by re-asserting Ephesus' claim to fame as beyond dispute. What is more to Luke's purpose, this public official declares the innocence of Gaius and Aristarchus of any crime while he reminds the excited audience that mob action against Christians is itself criminal.

Despite the mention of Gaius and Aristarchus the story does not bear too many marks of eye-witness testimony. We are struck again by the limited part Paul himself plays in the story, as indeed is true of much of the material Luke has gathered to sketch his outline of Paul's activity in Ephesus. From Paul's letters we are informed about many of the apostle's concerns in that time. Serious problems in the church in Corinth involved him on a "painful" (2 Cor 2:1) and abortive visit to that faction-torn community and repeated correspondence. The organisation of the great collection for the poor in Jerusalem took much of his energy, together with "the daily pressure of my anxiety for all the churches" (2 Cor 11:28). He writes in moving terms of "the affliction we experienced in Asia . . . we were so utterly, unbearably crushed that we despaired of life itself" (2 Cor 1:8-10; cf. 1 Cor 15:30-32), and may well have faced death in prison there.

Of this side of Paul's activity Luke makes no mention. In the march of the Gospel "to the ends of the earth" this chapter shows the "growth" of the word spreading from Ephesus through Asia. It subdues the dark power of magic, and undermines the great pagan religions, which are reduced to mindless repetition of ritual incantations in response to the mighty deeds of the apostle who integrates heterogeneous but connected religious groups into the unity of the Christian community. It is a picture of Paul at the height of his powers before he commences the last stage of the journey to Rome.

JOURNEY TO JERUSALEM. FROM EPHESUS TO TROAS. 20:1-6.

> **20** After the uproar ceased, Paul sent for the disciples and having exhorted them took leave of them and departed for Macedonia. [2]When he had gone through these parts and had given them much encouragement, he came to Greece. [3]There he spent three months, and when a plot was made against him by the Jews as he was about to set sail for Syria, he determined to return through Macedonia. [4]Sopater of Beroea, the son of Pyrrhus,

> accompanied him; and of the Thessalonians, Aristarchus and Secundus; and Gaius of Derbe, and Timothy; and the Asians, Tychicus and Trophimus. [5]These went on and were waiting for us at Troas, [6]but we sailed away from Philippi after the days of Unleavened Bread, and in five days we came to them at Troas, where we stayed for seven days.

The journey already announced in advance in 19:21 is dealt with in detail in 20:1-21:14. Once the journey is under way Luke seems to be drawing on a travel diary, the sparseness of whose details is enriched by episodes such as the miracle story about Eutychus (20:7-12), the discourse to the elders of Ephesus (20:18-38) and the prophecy of Agabus (21:10-11). But, as usual, Luke is master of the materials he is drawing on. The journey of the apostle to Jerusalem, which Paul's own letters show to be for the purpose of taking the collection (cf. Rom 15:25-27,31), becomes a replica of the journey of Jesus to his death and resurrection in Jerusalem. Just as the journey of Jesus is undertaken under divine necessity (Lk 13:33), marked by prophecies of suffering and death (e.g. Lk 9:51; 12:50; 13:33), and lack of understanding by his disciples, so, too, this journey of Paul is something that "must" be done (20:22; 21:13), despite prophetic warnings of what lies ahead (21:4,10-11) and the tears of friends who wish to discourage him (21:4,12-13).

Very quickly Luke sketches the journey through Macedonia (which includes such communities as Philippi, Thessalonica, Beroea) down to "Greece" or Achaia and Corinth. A Jewish conspiracy, probably to kill Paul at the port or on the journey, forces a change of plans from a sea voyage to Syria to a journey overland. Luke names a retinue of seven who we know from Paul's letters were representatives of their churches to take the collection to Jerusalem with Paul. Sopater of Beroea may be the Sosipater of Rom 16:21. Aristarchus and Gaius have already appeared in the riot in Ephesus. Secundus is an unknown representative of the church of Thessalonica. Timothy, too, has already appeared at work with Paul in Lycaonia (16:1). The representatives from the churches of Asia are the Ephesians Tychicus (mentioned in Col 4:7; Eph 6:21) and Trophimus, who will be the unsuspecting detonator of the fury of the Jerusalem Jews (Acts 21:29).

The "We-Sections" take up at v.5. Some of the group go on ahead to Troas, others go to Philippi till after the Passover before the company is reunited at Troas.

TROAS.
PAUL RAISES EUTYCHUS FROM THE DEAD.
20:7-12.

> [7]On the first day of the week, when we were gathered together to break bread, Paul talked with them, intending to depart on the morrow; and he prolonged his speech until midnight. [8]There were many lights in the upper chamber where we were gathered. [9]And a young man named Eutychus was sitting in the window. He sank into a deep sleep as Paul talked still longer; and being overcome by sleep, he fell down from the third story and was taken up dead. [10]But Paul went down and bent over him, and embracing him said, "Do not be alarmed, for his life is in him." [11]And when Paul had gone up and had broken bread and eaten, he conversed with them a long while, until daybreak, and so departed. [12]And they took the lad away alive, and were not a little comforted.

Luke has not previously mentioned the foundation of the church at Troas which "gathers together to break bread" on the first day of the week. (Verse 7, together with 1 Cor 16:2; Apoc 1:10, are the earliest attestations of the celebration of Sunday.) The miracle story that follows again parallels the activity of Paul with that of Peter (9:39-41) and their Lord (Lk 8:49-56).

In the course of the celebration of the Eucharist, Paul's protracted discourse and the atmosphere of the room cause

Eutychus (the name means "Lucky") to fall asleep and out of a third story window. Paul's gesture in lying on the dead youth and embracing him parallels that of the prophet Elijah (1 Kgs 17:21) and Elisha (2 Kgs 4:34). Luke sees the miracles as part of Paul's ministry of "encouragement" (v.12, cf. 20:1,2). His zeal unabated, the apostle continues till 5 a.m.

FROM TROAS TO MILETUS.
20:13-16.

> [13]But going ahead to the ship, we set sail for Assos, intending to take Paul aboard there; for so he had arranged, intending himself to go by land. [14]And when he met us at Assos, we took him on board and came to Mitylene. [15]And sailing from there we came the following day opposite Chios; the next day we touched at Samos; and the day after that we came to Miletus. [16]For Paul had decided to sail past Ephesus, so that he might not have to spend time in Asia; for he was hastening to be at Jerusalem, if possible, on the day of Pentecost.

These verses are hardly more than notes marking daily stopping places on the voyage. Why Paul travels overland rather than by boat round the promontory between Troas and Assos Luke does not explain. From Assos they travel to Mitylene on the island of Lesbos, then southwest to a point opposite the island of Chios, then to the island of Samos close to Ephesus which they bypass, probably for safety's sake, to gain the port of Miletus on the Asian coast at the mouth of the river Maeander.

DISCOURSE TO THE ELDERS OF EPHESUS.
20:17-38.

> [17]And from Miletus he sent to Ephesus and called to him the elders of the church. [18]And when they came to him, he said to them:
>
> "You yourselves know how I lived among you all the time from the first day that I set foot in Asia, [19]serving

the Lord with all humility and with tears and with trials which befell me through the plots of the Jews; [20]how I did not shrink from declaring to you anything that was profitable, and teaching you in public and from house to house, [21]testifying both to Jews and to Greeks of repentance to God and of faith in our Lord Jesus Christ. [22]And now, behold, I am going to Jerusalem, bound in the Spirit, not knowing what shall befall me there; [23]except that the Holy Spirit testifies to me in every city that imprisonment and afflictions await me. [24]But I do not account my life of any value nor as precious to myself, if only I may accomplish my course and the ministry which I received from the Lord Jesus, to testify to the gospel of the grace of God. [25]And now, behold, I know that all you among whom I have gone about preaching the kingdom will see my face no more. [26]Therefore I testify to you this day that I am innocent of the blood of all of you, [27]for I did not shrink from declaring to you the whole counsel of God. [28]Take heed to yourselves and to all the flock, in which the Holy Spirit has made you guardians, to feed the church of the Lord which he obtained with his own blood. [29]I know that after my departure fierce wolves will come in among you, not sparing the flock; [30]and from among your own selves will arise men speaking perverse things, to draw away the disciples after them. [31]Therefore be alert, remembering that for three years I did not cease night or day to admonish every one with tears. [32]And now I commend you to God and to the word of his grace, which is able to build you up and to give you the inheritance among all those who are sanctified. [33]I coveted no one's silver or gold or apparel. [34]You yourselves know that these hands ministered to my necessities, and to those who were with me. [35]In all things I have shown you that by so toiling one must help the weak, remembering the words of the Lord Jesus, how he said, 'It is more blessed to give than to receive.'"

> [36]And when he had spoken thus, he knelt down and prayed with them all. [37]And they all wept and embraced Paul and kissed him, [38]sorrowing most of all because of the word he had spoken, that they should see his face no more. And they brought him to the ship.

This third great discourse of Paul differs considerably in form and purpose from his missionary discourses to the Jews in Antioch of Pisidia (13:16-41) and to the Greeks at Athens (17:22-31). It is addressed to Christian pastors and comes as a conscious farewell to his missionary activity in Asia; it is simultaneously apologia and exhortation, Paul's last testament.

The discourse belongs to a literary form that is very well attested in the Bible. Israel's writers placed such discourses in the mouths of many great figures such as Moses (Deut 1-4; 31-33), Joshua (Josh 23-24) and the prophet Samuel (I Sam 12, with which this discourse shares some features). The manner and themes of these discourses are similar. At the end of their careers the speakers look back to the past and recall the great acts of the history of salvation to appeal to their people to "remember" them. They address themselves to the present in practical instructions, a defence of their own integrity and a call to imitate them, and utter prophecies for the future, often of infidelity to come. They include blessings and prayers and appeals to "serve the Lord." The later generations the writers address can find themselves in the situation predicted by their great forebear. The best known New Testament example of this form is John's final discourse of Jesus (Jn 13-17), but Luke had already anticipated him in the way he arranged his discourse of Jesus in the supper room (Lk 22:7-38).

Like the other discourses in Acts this is to be seen primarily as a work of Luke who arranges from materials available a discourse which presents Paul to his readers at the conclusion of his career, as the great missionary and pastor who speaks to Luke's own readers. The discourse can be filled out from Paul's own epistles, for it is replete with Pauline phrases.

The discourse is addressed to "elders" or presbyteroi, a title already given to leaders in Jewish communities and to groups of leaders of churches founded by Paul (cf. 14:23; 15:2,4,6 etc.; 16:4; 21:18). They are also addressed (v.28) as "overseers" or "guardians," in the Greek, *episkopoi*, a synonymous term. Though a number of units can be distinguished stylistically it is simplest to consider the material as falling into two main parts; in the first (vv.18-27) Paul speaks of himself and in the second (vv.28-38) of the duties of pastors.

The first section recalls Paul's past ministry in Ephesus (vv.18-21), registers his feeling about what lies ahead (vv.22-24), and, with his definitive separation in mind, testifies to his faithful accomplishment of his ministry (vv.25-27).

Of his ministry he recalls the way he shared their life completely, the "humility" (cf. Phil 2:3-4) that governed his conduct as "servant of the Lord" (cf. Rom 12:11; Col 3:24), the "tears" or anxieties brought on by unfaithful Christians (cf. 2 Cor 2:4; Phil 3:18) and "trials" or temptations that put his constancy to the test in the "plots of the Jews." (Luke has so far mentioned only one such "plot" in Acts 20:3, but the theme will recur in Jerusalem, 23:30). He hid nothing from them, drew back from nothing in his mission to "Jews and Greeks," calling them to "repentance" (Lk 24:47; Acts 5:31; 11:18) and "faith in the Lord Jesus" (cf. Acts 24:24).

As for what lies ahead, Paul speaks as if he already considers himself a prisoner, "bound in the Spirit," led to Jerusalem by the same power as has directed his whole ministry. Verse 23 is illustrated by the episodes to follow in Tyre and Caesarea (21:4,10-11). All that matters is that he can "finish my race" (cf. 2 Tim 4:7; Phil 2:16) and fulfil the ministry "received from the Lord Jesus"(cf. 2 Cor 3:6; 5:18-19).

With his separation from them in mind Paul points to his duty fully accomplished. The nature of the speech as a farewell is underlined by the repetition of v.25 in the conclusion (v.38), just as v.27 repeats the theme of v.20 and thus reaffirms Paul's fidelity to his task. He has revealed to them "the whole plan of God," the work which God Himself is realising and the conditions on which men will profit by it (cf. 2:23; 4:28; 5:38; 13:36). Whatever evil happens in the future is no fault of Paul's.

The second section addresses itself to pastors and their duties. It deals with the sacredness of the charge they have received (v.28), the dangers threatening the flock that demand vigilance (vv.29-31), commends the pastors to God (v.32) and closes on a final recommendation to disinterestedness (vv.33-35).

The sacredness of their charge is underlined in that they have been established in their pastoral ministry by the Holy Spirit (cf. 1 Cor 12:28; Eph 4:11; Acts 13:2-4) and that the people they care for are "the church of God" (cf. 1 Thess 2:14; 1 Cor 1:2). The final phrase of v.28 is unusual. Manuscript readings vary between "with his own blood," "with the blood of his Own," or make the phrase refer to Christ. What is being emphasized is that the church is God's special possession (cf. Eph 1:14; 1 Pet 2:9), acquired as His covenant people by the death of Christ.

The dangers threatening the flock are described in conventional terms. "Fierce wolves" are false teachers (Mt 7:15), who threaten even from inside the community. Paul's own example now becomes a model for their conduct. As becomes the departing leader he commends them to God (as in 14:23), whose "word of grace" can "build up" the community in the present (Rom 16:25; Eph 1:14,18) and bring it to its heavenly goal. Paul's final exhortation, again based on his own example (cf. 1 Sam 12:3-4), is to be selfless as he is and to care for the weak. He closes with an otherwise unknown saying of Jesus regarding the blessings of generosity.

FROM MILETUS TO JERUSALEM. 21:1-14.

21 And when we had parted from them and set sail, we came by a straight course to Cos, and the next day to Rhodes, and from there to Patara. [2]And having found a ship crossing to Phoenicia, we went aboard, and set sail. [3]When we had come in sight of Cyprus, leaving it on the left we sailed to Syria, and landed at Tyre; for there the ship was to unload its cargo. [4]And having sought out the disciples, we stayed there for seven days. Through the Spirit they told Paul not to go on to Jerusalem. [5]And when our days there were ended, we departed and went on our journey; and they all, with wives and children, brought us on our way till we were outside the city; and kneeling down on the beach we prayed and bade one another farewell. [6]Then we went on board the ship, and they returned home.

[7]When we had finished the voyage from Tyre, we arrived at Ptolemiais; and we greeted the brethren and stayed with them for one day. [8]On the morrow we departed and came to Caesarea; and we entered the house of Philip the evangelist, who was one of the seven, and stayed with him. [9]And he had four unmarried daughters, who prophesied. [10]While we were staying for some days, a prophet named Agabus came down form Judea. [11]And coming to us he took Paul's girdle and bound his own feet and hands, and said, "Thus says the Holy Spirit, 'So shall the Jews at Jerusalem bind the man who owns this girdle and deliver him into the hands of the Gentiles.'" [12]When we heard this, we and the people there begged him not to go up to Jerusalem. [13]Then Paul answered, "What are you doing, weeping and breaking my heart? For I am ready not only to be imprisoned but even to die at Jerusalem for the name of the Lord Jesus." [14]And when he would not be persuaded, we ceased and said, "The will of the Lord be done."

The travel diary style resumes. Three short stages from Miletus to the island of Cos, then to the island of Rhodes and the Asian sea port of Patara are followed by the much longer Mediterranean journey southeast to the Palestinian coast at Tyre. The prophetic warnings of the community cannot divert Paul from his destination and this community, too, engages in a moving farewell as it escorts him to the boat. There is another brief stay with the community at Ptolemais, twenty-seven miles south on the Phoenician coast, before the last stop at Caesarea. Luke heightens the feeling of impending doom with his story of the prophecy of Agabus. Although the household of Philip (cf. 8:40) is amply blessed with women prophets it is the prophet who had previously predicted the famine in Jerusalem (11:27-29) who speaks. After the manner of the classical prophets (cf. Is 20:2-6; Jer 13:1-11; Ezek 4:1-17) Agabus acts out his prophecy, taking the long cloth Paul used and binding his own feet and hands. His prophecy is comparable to Jesus' prophecy of his Passion (cf. Mk 10:33; Lk 9:44). For a last time the request "not to go up to Jerusalem" is heard (v.12, cf. v.4). But Paul is undeterred; he is after all, already "bound in the Spirit" and prepared to follow his Lord even to death. The prayer "the will of the Lord be done" echoes that of Jesus (Lk 22:42).

SECTION 3.
FROM JERUSALEM TO ROME.
21:15 - 28:31.

Paul's arrival in Jerusalem begins the last section of Luke's two volume book. The direction has been indicated in advance in 19:21 and the repeated warnings as to what lies ahead alert the reader to the significance of the opening sentence "After these days we made ready and went up to Jerusalem" (21:15). A decisive moment has been reached.

It seems as if the wheel has come full circle back to Jerusalem where the action commenced and, in fact, Paul now speaks to the Jews in Jerusalem as had Peter. Just as the Sadducees had been disturbed by Peter's "proclaiming in Jesus the resurrection from the dead" (4:2), so now this theme is taken up and fully developed by Paul. He claims that it is precisely for this belief that he is on trial (23:6) and the Roman official Festus rightly assesses the heart of the controversy as concerning "one Jesus, who was dead, but whom Paul asserted to be alive" (25:19).

Luke continues to parallel the career of Paul with that of Jesus in a conscious fashion throughout this section. In a series of details the life of the apostle imitates that of his Master. Like Jesus on his arrival in Jerusalem Paul is well received and the Jewish-Christian community praise God for his deeds (21:17-20 cf. Lk 19:37). He goes to the Temple (21:26 cf. Lk 19:45-48), encounters disbelief from the Sadducees on the matter of the resurrection but support from the scribes (23:6-9 cf. Lk 20:27-39). He is seized by a mob (21:30 cf. Lk 22:63-64), struck at the high priest's command (23:2 cf. Lk 22:63-64), declared innocent three times (23:9; 25:25-26:31 cf. Lk 23:4,14,22).

The section falls naturally into three parts. The first (21:15-40) concerns Paul's reception in Jerusalem, appearance in the Temple and arrest. It can be regarded as a long introduction to the discourse that follows. The second consists of chapters 22-26, centering on three discourses which represent three statements by Paul of his position before different groups of people. He is a prisoner throughout, engaged in what amounts to one continuous dispute with Judaism. In the course of this he appeals to Caesar (25:11), which brings about his voyage to Rome and his ministry there which conclude the two volumes (27-28).

The story is lively and exciting; Luke the story teller is at his best. But the major feature of the whole section is the discourses at beginning and close. Formal speeches make up practically one third of this section and, if dialogue is added, the proportion reaches nearly one half. The discourses differ in form and function from the missionary discourses of earlier chapters. They are in the first person; Paul is speaking in self-defence (22:1; 24:10; 25:8; 26:1,24). They do not fit precisely the historical situation in which they are placed or respond to the historical circumstances Paul is speaking of in the charges he is answering, a reminder that Luke is telling the story of the apostle not as historical recitation but as response to the concerns and questions of his readers.

PAUL'S RECEPTION BY THE JEWISH CHRISTIANS IN JERUSALEM. 21:15-26.

> [15]After these days we made ready and went up to Jerusalem. [16]And some of the disciples from Caesarea went with us, bringing us to the house of Mnason of Cyprus, an early disciple, with whom we should lodge.
>
> [17]When we had come to Jerusalem, the brethren received us gladly. [18]On the following day Paul went in with us to James; and all the elders were present. [19]After greeting them, he related one by one the things that God had done among the Gentiles through his ministry. [20]And when they heard it, they glorified God. And they said to him, "You see, brother, how many thousands there are among the Jews of those who have believed; they are all

> zealous for the law, [21]and they have been told about you that you teach all the Jews who are among the Gentiles to forsake Moses, telling them not to circumcise their children or observe the customs. [22]What then is to be done? They will certainly hear that you have come. [23]Do therefore what we tell you. We have four men who are under a vow; [24]take these men and purify yourself along with them and pay their expenses, so that they may shave their heads. Thus all will know that there is nothing in what they have been told about you but that you yourself live in observance of the law. [25]But as for the Gentiles who have believed, we have sent a letter with our judgment that they should abstain from what has been sacrificed to idols and from blood and from what is strangled and from unchastity." [26]Then Paul took the men, and the next day he purified himself with them and went into the temple, to give notice when the days of purification would be fulfilled and the offering presented for every one of them.

Where Paul writes of his own concerns in the visit to Jerusalem he asks prayers that he "be delivered from the unbelievers in Judea" and also that the collection which he and the delegates of the Gentile churches were taking "may be acceptable to the saints" (Rom 15:31). Luke's story makes no mention of the collection (cf. 24:17). This episode shows Paul and his companions warmly received by James and the Jewish Christian community. The following story shows how well-grounded were Paul's fears.

Paul's host in Jerusalem is Mnason, one of the early disciples, a Cypriot like Barnabas, possibly a Hellenist. From his house Paul and his companions go to visit James. Peter has long since disappeared from Luke's story. James is leader of the community and Luke perhaps suggests a distinction between him and "all the elders," who do not seem to play the same part, under his leadership, as "the elders" of Ephesus after Paul's departure.

For the third time the Jerusalem community "glorifies God" for "the things that God had done among the Gentiles," and a second time for the ministry of Paul (11:18; 15:12). But they also tell of the success of the Christian mission to the Jews in Jerusalem. Luke's exaggeration of the numbers ("How many tens of thousands") only increases the pathos of this remark, made only ten years before the destruction of Jerusalem and the dispersal of the Jewish Christian community. All these are ardent observers of the Law, and what they have heard of Paul's teaching is that it obliges Jews living in Gentile lands to "apostasy" from the law of Moses. Paul would not have recognised his teaching in the propositions they list, "to forsake Moses, not to circumcise their children or observe the customs" (v.21), though phrases in the epistle to the Galatians could easily be distorted in this way.

James suggests that Paul associate himself with four devout Jewish members of the community in a gesture that will establish his solidarity with their feeling about the Law and the Temple and his own bona fides as a devout Jew. Some of the details of this gesture are difficult to determine and suggest a confusion on Luke's own part due to lack of precise information. Paul is to pay the expenses of the sacrificial offerings involved in the completion of the Nazirite vow (cf. Num 6:1-21) for four members of the community, a not inconsiderable sum. This much is clear; the purpose of Paul's own seven day "purification" is not. He cannot be fulfilling a similar vow which required a minimum of thirty days. Luke may think of it as a ritual purification for a Jew returning from abroad. In Luke's story, however, it is Paul's compliance with James' suggestion of a gesture which places him regularly in the Temple that leads to Paul's arrest. There is no further mention of James and his community in Acts. Verse 25 seems to inform Paul of the decree of the Council (15:20) as if he knew nothing of it, but its purpose in the story is to refer to Paul's Gentile friends of whom no such signs of conformity with the Law are demanded, only the observance of the four basic regulations.

ARREST OF PAUL IN THE TEMPLE. 21:27-36.

> [27]When the seven days were almost completed, the Jews from Asia, who had seen him in the temple, stirred up all the crowd, and laid hands on him, [28]crying out, "Men of Israel, help! This is the man who is teaching men everywhere against the people and the law and this place; moreover he also brought Greeks into the temple, and he has defiled this holy place." [29]For they had previously seen Trophimus the Ephesian with him in the city, and they supposed that Paul had brought him into the temple. [30]Then all the city was aroused, and the people ran together; they seized Paul and dragged him out of the temple, and at once the gates were shut. [31]And as they were trying to kill him, word came to the tribune of the cohort that all Jerusalem was in confusion. [32]He at once took soldiers and centurions, and ran down to them; and when they saw the tribune and the soldiers, they stopped beating Paul. [33]Then the tribune came up and arrested him, and ordered him to be bound with two chains. He inquired who he was and what he had done. [34]Some in the crowd shouted one thing, some another; and as he could not learn the facts because of the uproar, he ordered him to be brought into the barracks. [35]And when he came to the steps, he was actually carried by the soldiers because of the violence of the crowd; [36]for the mob of the people followed, crying, "Away with him!"

Paul is recognised in the Temple by Jews from Ephesus who seize him and start a riot. Their accusation against Paul of "teaching men everywhere against the people and the law and this place" resembles the charge against Stephen (6:13), the charge of "defiling this holy place" recurs in 24:5-6. Gentiles were permitted in the large outer court of the

Temple, but the low stone wall which separated the Court of the Gentiles from the court of Israel, the next inner area, carried warnings in Greek and Latin reminding Gentiles of the penalty of death for trespassing there. The exaggeration of the story-teller enters into the remark that "the whole city" was aroused. The temple guards anticipate violence and close the gates separating the two courts while the mob attempts to lynch Paul.

It was to obviate this kind of situation, particularly at the time of the great feasts, as well as to deter religiously-inspired movements leading to revolt, that the Romans stationed a garrison in the fortress Antonia at the north-western corner of the Temple. The intervention of the Romans (tribune, centurions and soldiers) saves Paul who is arrested and "bound with two chains." The prophecy of Agabus is already fulfilled (21:11); from this point to the end of the story Paul is a prisoner. No worthwhile information can be obtained from the crowd since it is Paul who is about to speak for himself. The crowd calls for the death of Paul as they had for that of Jesus (cf. Lk 23:18).

PAUL'S DEFENCE BEFORE THE JEWISH PEOPLE. "I AM A JEW . . ." 21:37 - 22:21.

[37]As Paul was about to be brought into the barracks, he said to the tribune, "May I say something to you?" And he said, "Do you know Greek? [38]Are you not the Egyptian, then, who recently stirred up a revolt and led the four thousand men of the Assassins out into the wilderness?" [39]Paul replied, "I am a Jew, from Tarsus in Cilicia, a citizen of no mean city; I beg you, let me speak to the people." [40]And when he had given him leave, Paul, standing on the steps, motioned with his hands to the people; and when there was a great hush, he spoke to them in the Hebrew language, saying:

22 "Brethren and fathers, hear the defence which I now make before you."

[2]And when they heard that he addressed them in the Hebrew language, they were the more quiet. And he said:

[3]"I am a Jew, born at Tarsus in Cilicia, but brought up in this city at the feet of Gamaliel, educated according to the strict manner of the law of our fathers, being zealous for God as you all are this day. [4]I persecuted this Way to the death, binding and delivering to prison both men and women, [5]as the high priest and the whole council of elders bear me witness. From them I received letters to the brethren, and I journeyed to Damascus to take those also who were there and bring them in bonds to Jerusalem to be punished.

[6]"As I made my journey and drew near to Damascus, about noon a great light from heaven suddenly shone about me. [7]And I fell to the ground and heard a voice saying to me, 'Saul, Saul, why do you persecute me?' [8]And I answered, 'Who are you, Lord?' And he said to me, 'I am Jesus of Nazareth whom you are persecuting.' [9]Now those who were with me saw the light but did not hear the voice of the one who was speaking to me. [10]And I said, 'What shall I do, Lord?' And the Lord said to me, 'Rise, and go into Damascus, and there you will be told all that is appointed for you to do.' [11]And when I could not see because of the brightness of that light, I was led by the hand by those who were with me, and came into Damascus.

[12]"And one Ananias, a devout man according to the law, well spoken of by all the Jews who lived there, [13]came to me, and standing by me said to me, 'Brother Saul, receive your sight.' And in that very hour I received my sight and saw him. [14]And he said, 'The God of our fathers appointed you to know his will, to see the Just One and to hear a voice from his mouth; [15]for you will be a witness for him to all men of what you have seen and heard. [16]And now why do you wait? Rise and be baptized, and wash away your sins, calling on his name.'

> [17]"When I had returned to Jerusalem and was praying in the temple, I fell into a trance [18]and saw him saying to me, 'Make haste and get quickly out of Jerusalem, because they will not accept your testimony about me.' [19]And I said, 'Lord, they themselves know that in every synagogue I imprisoned and beat those who believed in thee. [20]And when the blood of Stephen thy witness was shed, I also was standing by and approving, and keeping the garments of those who killed him.' [21]And he said to me, 'Depart; for I will send you far away to the Gentiles.'"

Chapters 22-26 form a connected unit, built around discourses of Paul which are very similar in occasion, context and content (22:1-21; 22:30 - 23:11; 26:1-32). These really make up one progressively developing discourse, a continuing defence carried on before different judges. In each of them Paul defends his Jewish orthodoxy, his preaching of the resurrection of the dead and his mission to the Gentiles, though the terms of Paul's creed become more explicit as the story progresses.

The setting for the first discourse (vv.37-40) is Luke's work. In the midst of the tumult, as he is being carried up the steps in chains and under the protective custody of the soldiers, Paul addresses the tribune deferentially in Greek with a request to make a speech to the mob that is clamouring for his death. The centurion, promptly reassured by the briefest of dialogues that Paul is a law-abiding citizen, grants his request and Paul's opening oratorical gesture reduces the crowd to silence. This is not the stuff of history, but an introduction Luke has fashioned for his own purposes.

The tribune's response lumps together several distinct episodes of recent history recorded by Josephus, the activity of the Sicarii or assassins, marches into the desert inspired by self-styled prophets anticipating God's liberation, and an Egyptian who led 4000 people from the desert to await on the Mount of Olives the fall of the walls of Jerusalem. The dialogue and the ensuing permission of the tribune show that Paul is no part of these dangerous and seditious movements that threaten the peace of the Roman empire, but an authentic Jew and a Roman citizen. His discourse thus comes as the self defence of a law-abiding and authentic Jew to the Jewish people in their mother tongue in the centre of Judaism.

The discourse rehearses Paul's Jewish upbringing and activity as a persecutor (vv.3-5), tells the story of his Conversion (vv.6-16) and his vision in the Temple (vv.17-21). As it progresses the reader notes that Paul is defending himself uniquely against the sweeping charges of 21:28. His orthodox upbringing and the piety of the Jewish Ananias who introduced him to the Damascus community suggest his respect for the Jewish people and the Law. The accusation of defiling the Temple by introducing the Gentile Trophimus is not countered at all. The thrust of the speech is to show the lawfulness of the mission to the Gentiles, commenced at God's direction, by an explicit command of the risen Christ, while Paul was at prayer in the Temple itself.

"I am a Jew" (repeated from v.39), is a basic assertion (cf. 23:6; 24:14). Paul is no renegade; Christianity implies no apostasy from Judaism. Born, brought up, educated as a Jew, a persecutor of "this Way," how could he have come to his present beliefs? Only if God had intervened, as the rest of the speech illustrates.

This second account of his conversion is briefer than the first (9:3-19), which it presupposes and from which it differs in details, most of which can be ascribed to Luke's search for variety and the nature of the audience Paul is addressing. Ananias, previously "a disciple" (9:10), is here depicted as a devout Jew, "well spoken of by all the Jews living there." Paul's mission is stated in more Jewish terms (v.14). It comes from "the God of our fathers," whose "will" or plan of salvation is revealed to Paul. Jesus is "the Just One" (cf. 3:14; 7:52). At the same time Paul's role as "witness" shows him as a continuer of the work of the Twelve (1:8; 10:41), not of course, a witness to the earthly Jesus as they were but to "what you have seen and heard," the Risen Jesus and the work of the Spirit in the mission.

In the previous account (9:26-30) Luke described Paul's return to Jerusalem and his departure because of a Jewish plot to kill him. In this version his departure is made at the command of the Risen Lord. The discourse proceeds to its climax with Paul's account of a vision in the Temple itself. The dialogue between the Risen Lord and Paul brings out the incongruity of Paul's rejection by the Jews, not only in the beginning but, as the reader knows, through his whole missionary career (13:46-48; 18:6; 28:25-28). So far Paul's mission has only been stated as "for all men." At the explicit mention of "the Gentiles" he is brought to a halt by the response of the hitherto silent crowd.

PAUL THE ROMAN CITIZEN.
22:22-29.

[22]Up to this word they listened to him; then they lifted up their voices and said, "Away with such a fellow from the earth! For he ought not to live," [23]And as they cried out and waved their garments and threw dust into the air, [24]the tribune commanded him to be brought into the barracks, and ordered him to be examined by scourging, to find out why they shouted thus against him. [25]But when they had tied him up with the thongs, Paul said to the centurion who was standing by, "Is it lawful for you to scourge a man who is a Roman citizen, and uncondemned?" [26]When the centurion heard that, he went to the tribune and said to him, "What are you about to do? For this man is a Roman citizen." [27]So the tribune came and said to him, "Tell me, are you a Roman citizen?" And he said, "Yes." [28]The tribune answered, "I bought

this citizenship for a large sum." Paul said, "But I was born a citizen." [29]So those who were about to examine him withdrew from him instantly; and the tribune also was afraid, for he realised that Paul was a Roman citizen and that he had bound him.

The truth of the Lord's words, "They will not accept your testimony about me," (v.18) is borne out in the reaction of the crowd to Paul's mention of his mission to the Gentiles. Luke's story is at its liveliest; he has switched the crowd off for Paul's speech; now he switches it on to fever pitch as it repeats and enlarges its previous demand for Paul's death (21:36). The tribune, too, is suddenly devoid of the assurance in Paul that had permitted his speech in the first place. With deliberate suspense Luke leaves the revelation of Paul's Roman citizenship to the last moment when Paul, stretched out on a bench ready for scourging, puts the question which changes the tune entirely. It was one thing to obtain information under torture from slaves; the ominous question "Is it lawful to scourge a man who is a Roman citizen, and that before trial?" reminds all concerned that Paul is no anonymous miscreant and that the direst penalties await such treatment in his case. The word passes from centurion to tribune and reduces him to an attitude of proper respect. Paul has taken the initiative away from the Roman official.

PAUL BEFORE THE SANHEDRIN. 22:30 - 23:11.

[30]But on the morrow, desiring to know the real reason why the Jews accused him, he unbound him, and commanded the chief priests and all the council to meet, and he brought Paul down and set him before them.
23 And Paul, looking intently at the council, said, "Brethren, I have lived before God in all good conscience up to this day." [2]And the high priest Ananias commanded

> those who stood by him to strike him on the mouth. [3]Then Paul said to him, "God shall strike you, you whitewashed wall! Are you sitting to judge me according to the law, and yet contrary to the law you order me to be struck?" [4]Those who stood by said, "Would you revile God's high priest?" [5]And Paul said, "I did not know, brethren, that he was the high priest; for it is written, 'You shall not speak evil of a ruler of your people.'"
>
> [6]But when Paul perceived that one part were Sadducees and the other Pharisees, he cried out in the council, "Brethren, I am a Pharisee, a son of Pharisees; with respect to the hope and the resurrection of the dead I am on trial." [7]And when he had said this, a dissension arose between the Pharisees and the Sadducees; and the assembly was divided. [8]For the Sadducees say that there is no resurrection, nor angel, nor spirit; but the Pharisees acknowledge them all. [9]Then a great clamour arose; and some of the scribes of the Pharisees' party stood up and contended. "We find nothing wrong in this man. What if a spirit or an angel spoke to him?" [10]And when the dissension became violent, the tribune, afraid that Paul would be torn in pieces by them, commanded the soldiers to go down and take him by force from among them and bring him into the barracks.
>
> [11]The following night the Lord stood by him and said, "Take courage, for as you have testified about me at Jerusalem, so you must bear witness also at Rome."

Like the Jewish Christians before them the Jewish crowd now disappear from the pages of Acts. Paul's self defence is next conducted before the Jewish leaders, first of all before the Sanhedrin. So far the Roman official has not succeeded in obtaining any worth-while information about any crime of Paul's (a point Luke makes repeatedly in this section, cf. 22:30; 23:28; 25:20,26), so he summons the Sanhedrin into session.

A sufficient number of details are historically unlikely in this story to suggest that the construction of the scene is very much the work of Luke. Admittedly the law forbade the tribune to interrogate Paul under torture, but he makes no attempt to ask him any further questions. Instead he summons the highest Jewish court into session to know "the real reason why the Jews accused him." The commander of the Roman forces in Jerusalem had no power to summon the Sanhedrin far less, as a pagan, was his presence there (together with some soldiers) likely to be tolerated. The session, intended as a search for information, turns into a trial of Paul (v.6), who speaks without being called (v.1) and does not even recognise the high priest (v.5). Pharisees and Sadducees, reconciled for ages to working together despite their known differences of belief, are violently divided by Paul's introduction of a topic on which they differ. Taken together with other items these inconsistencies justify the conclusion that Luke had very little precise information about the occasion and that he has constructed a representative scene to show his readers the basic reasons for the differences dividing Christianity from Judaism in his own time.

Paul experiences the fate of which Jesus had warned His disciples: "they will lay their hands on you and persecute you, delivering you up to the synagogues and prisons, and you will be brought before kings and governors for my name's sake" (Lk 21:12). Like Peter and John before him (4:5-22; 5:27-39), Paul stands on trial before the Sanhedrin in imitation of his Lord (Lk 22:66-71).

The scene is symmetrically arranged with two parts balancing one another (22:30-23:5; 23:6-10). Each commences with an address to the audience and a statement of innocence or orthodoxy by Paul which is followed by a violent reaction on the part of his audience. In earlier days Paul had enjoyed the favour of these authorities in his activities as persecutor. At his first declaration of innocence he is struck on the mouth at the command of the high priest Ananias (cf. Jn 18:22). Though Paul's response rings out as a curse and is hardly in accord with the rule of apostolic conduct spelled out in 1 Cor 4:12, it is also prophetic of Ananias' death at the hands of assassins some six years later. In his violation of the Law by which alone he is empowered to judge, the high priest is a "whited wall," a model of the hyprocisy slated by Jesus (Mt 23:27).

Paul goes further than his general protestation of innocence. He claims he remains an orthodox Pharisee; and it is this claim that divides the Sadducees, the members of the priestly families, and the scribes who were mainly Pharisees. With v.6 a central statement is reached. Paul claims that what the trial is really about is the Pharisaic "hope of the resurrection of the dead." Paul claims that his message is not at all contrary to Judaism; it is the fulfilment of the dearest hopes of his people in the very form articulated by the Pharisees. This claim will be reiterated and developed in subsequent speeches (24:14-15; 26:6,7,22-23). Luke explains the difference between the two sects for the benefit of his reader (v.8). That the Sadducees denied the existence of angels and spirits is not otherwise attested. The Pharisees take Paul's side. Their remark, "What if a spirit or an angel spoke to him?" admits the possibility of divine inspiration in his mission.

Luke shows his readers that their belief is continuous with the belief of the Pharisaic strand in Judaism. The Christian faith is not a denial of Judaism but the fulfilment of its Messianic aspirations. Were the Pharisees to listen carefully to the Christian message they would acknowledge this. Their beliefs force them to consider the possibility that even the mission to the Gentiles that has culminated in the church of Luke's day may be a legitimate, valid, even divinely inspired continuation of the faith of Israel. The story also prepares the ground for Paul's appeal to Rome. He cannot hope for justice in proceedings before the official representatives of his people.

Paul's vision (v.11) rounds out the scene. It is both reassurance of protection and a reminder to the reader (like 19:21) that the course events are to take is not dictated by the "plot" of the Jews. The plan of God directs Paul's course to Rome as he takes the first step in his journey to Caesarea.

THE PLOT OF THE JEWS.
23:12-35.

[12]When it was day, the Jews made a plot and bound themselves by an oath neither to eat nor drink till they had killed Paul. [13]There were more than forty who made this conspiracy. [14]And they went to the chief priests and elders, and said, "We have strictly bound ourselves by an oath to taste no food till we have killed Paul. [15]You therefore, along with the council, give notice now to the tribune to bring him down to you, as though you were going to determine his case more exactly. And we are ready to kill him before he comes near."

[16]Now the son of Paul's sister heard of their ambush; so he went and entered the barracks and told Paul. [17]And Paul called one of the centurions and said, "Bring this young man to the tribune; for he has something to tell him." [18]So he took him and brought him to the tribune and said, "Paul the prisoner called me and asked me to bring this young man to you, as he has something to say to you." [19]The tribune took him by the hand, and going aside asked him privately, "What is it that you have to tell me?" [20]And he said, "The Jews have agreed to ask you to bring Paul down to the council tomorrow, as though they were going to inquire somewhat more closely about him. [21]But do not yield to them; for more than forty of their men lie in ambush for him, having bound themselves by an oath neither to eat nor drink till they have killed him; and now they are ready, waiting for the promise from you." [22]So the tribune dismissed the young man, charging him, "Tell no one that you have informed me of this."

[23]Then he called two of the centurions and said, "At the third hour of the night get ready two hundred soldiers with seventy horsemen and two hundred spearmen to go as far as Caesarea. [24]Also provide mounts for Paul to ride, and bring him safely to Felix the governor." [25]And he wrote a letter to this effect.

[26]"Claudius Lysias to his Excellency the governor Felix, greeting. [27]This man was seized by the Jews, and was about to be killed by them, when I came upon them with the soldiers and rescued him, having learned that he was a Roman citizen. [28]And desiring to know the charge on which they accused him, I brought him down to their council. [29]I found that he was accused about questions of their law, but charged with nothing deserving death or imprisonment. [30]And when it was disclosed to me that there would be a plot against the man, I sent him to you at once, ordering his accusers also to state before you what they have against him."

[31]So the soldiers, according to their instructions, took Paul and brought him by night to Antipatris. [32]And on the morrow they returned to the barracks, leaving the horsemen to go on with him. [33]When they came to Caesarea and delivered the letter to the governor, they presented Paul also before him. [34]On reading the letter, he asked to what province he belonged. When he learned that he was from Cilicia [35]he said, "I will hear you when your accusers arrive." And he commanded him to be guarded in Herod's praetorium.

Again Luke makes the most of his material to construct a lively story. He repeats events he has already narrated (vv.26-30) as well as providing the new details (vv.12-13, 14,20-21). Paul's first move towards his ultimate destination does not make a particularly "religious" story except as an instance of God's providential care of his witness. What it illustrates more clearly is the animosity of "the Jews," more specifically of certain members of the Sandhedrin, the innocence of Paul, and the attitude of the Roman authorities in this third example of their efforts to save Paul from his countrymen.

A bunch of forty conspirators bind themselves by solemn oath to kill Paul. They approach the Sanhedrin and propose a plan which will profit by the centurion's known desire for information. Paul's nephew has no trouble visiting his uncle in jail, and Paul has little trouble in persuading the centurion to take the youth to the tribune. The military commander of Jerusalem is a model of kindness, takes him by the hand out of earshot, accepts his information with remarkable trust, and with due security precautions arranges for a most impressive bodyguard to safeguard Paul not only in the streets of Jerusalem where it seems the attempt is to be made but all the way to Caesarea. Half his garrison set out immediately, at nine o'clock at night. Paul arrives at Caesarea, where, after a preliminary hearing before the procurator, he is kept under guard in the praetorium. The letter of Lysias which not unnaturally places his own conduct in the most favourable light repeats the previous judgment of Gallio in Paul's earlier confrontation with the Jews in Corinth (18:15). The attitude of this Roman official to the controversies between Paul and the Jews is that it simply concerns "questions of their law" and that Paul has been "charged with nothing that deserves death or imprisonment."

TRIAL BEFORE FELIX.
24:1-23.

> **24** And after five days the high priest Ananias came down with some elders and a spokesman, one Tertullus. They laid before the governor their case against Paul; [2]and when he was called, Tertullus began to accuse him, saying:

"Since through you we enjoy much peace, and since by your provision, most excellent Felix, reforms are introduced on behalf of this nation, [3]in every way and everywhere we accept this with all gratitude. [4]But, to detain you no further, I beg you in your kindness to hear us briefly. [5]For we have found this man a pestilent fellow, an agitator among all the Jews, throughout the world, and a ringleader of the sect of the Nazarenes. [6]He even tried to profane the temple, but we seized him. [8]By examining him yourself you will be able to learn from him about everything of which we accuse him."

[9]The Jews also joined in the charge, affirming that all this was so.

[10]And when the governor had motioned to him to speak, Paul replied:

"Realising that for many years you have been judge over this nation, I cheerfully make my defence. [11]As you may ascertain, it is not more than twelve days since I went up to worship at Jerusalem; [12]and they did not find me disputing with any one or stirring up a crowd, either in the temple or in the synagogues, or in the city. [13]Neither can they prove to you what they now bring up against me. [14]But this I admit to you, that according to the Way, which they call a sect, I worship the God of our fathers, believing everything laid down by the law or written in the prophets, [15]having a hope in God which these themselves accept, that there will be a resurrection of both the just and the unjust. [16]So I always take pains to have a clear conscience toward God and toward men. [17]Now after some years I came to bring to my nation alms and offerings. [18]As I was doing this, they found me purified in the temple, without any crowd or tumult. But some Jews from Asia—[19]they ought to be here before you and to make an accusation, if they have anything against me. [20]Or else let these men themselves say what wrongdoing they found when I stood before the council,

[21]except this one thing which I cried out while standing among them, 'With respect to the resurrection of the dead I am on trial before you this day.'"

[22]But Felix, having a rather accurate knowledge of the Way, put them off, saying, "When Lysias the tribune comes down, I will decide your case." [23]Then he gave orders to the centurion that he should have some liberty, and that none of his friends should be prevented from attending to his needs.

The next stage in the continuing controversy is a legal trial. Paul confronts his adversaries before the Roman governor of the province. Felix was a successor of Pontius Pilate in the succession of Roman procurators entrusted with the civil and military administration of Judaea. Roman historians do not subscribe to the flattering estimate of Felix's career with which the rhetor Tertullus commenced his harangue according to the conventions of his profession (v.2) before formulating the Jewish charges against Paul. Paul "stirs up strife" among Jews the world over, he is "ringleader of the sect of the Nazoreans" (the only place in the New Testament where this term is used), and he has profaned the Temple.

Paul's obligatory opening flattery is briefer and closer to the facts, for Felix's career had offered ample opportunity to familiarise himself with Jewish ways. Paul disposes of the first charge, that of inciting to riot, by pointing to the brief time he has been in Jerusalem in which, as the governor can readily inform himself, he has not engaged in disputes "either in the temple or in the synagogue, or in the city." This is a matter of public record. As to what his enemies call "the sect of the Nazoreans," Paul declines the term and any pejorative overtones it may have by calling it "the Way" (cf. 19:9,23). Again he insists on its continuity with Judaism in its worship of the same God, belief in the same Law and prophets. He re-states "the hope of the resurrection of the dead" for pagan ears as "the resurrection of the just and the unjust" (v.15), a belief that obliges him to "a clear conscience toward God and toward men." The remaining charge he meets by insisting on his conduct as a devout Jew. He had come to worship in Jerusalem (v.11), bringing alms for his people (v.17, Luke's only reference to the collection) and engaged in the ritual of Jewish purification when seized by a group of Asian Jews who, far from bringing any accusation against him, are not even in court. Those accusers who are present can only testify to his proclamation of the resurrection.

The end result is neither acquittal nor condemnation but adjournment, with a lessening of the constraints of Paul's custody. It is not a complete victory, but the governor of the province has found nothing criminal in his activity.

PAUL AND FELIX.
24:24-27.

> [24]After some days Felix came with his wife Drusilla, who was a Jewess; and he sent for Paul and heard him speak upon faith in Christ Jesus. [25]And as he argued about justice and self-control and future judgment, Felix was alarmed and said, "Go away for the present; when I have an opportunity I will summon you." [26]At the same time he hoped that money would be given him by Paul. So he sent for him often and conversed with him. [27]But when two years had elapsed, Felix was succeeded by Porcius Festus; and desiring to do the Jews a favour, Felix left Paul in prison.

Luke explains the reason for Paul's two year imprisonment in Caesarea and offers a summary of the Christian message as proclaimed to a pagan official well disposed to the apostle. The Roman governor is accompanied by his wife Drusilla in a scene reminiscent of the story of Herod Antipas and John the Baptist (Mk 6:17-20). The interest of Drusilla is explained by the fact that she is a Jewess, though her matrimonial status at the time qualified her as anything but devout. The youngest daughter of Agrippa I, she had previously been married to the king of Emesa in Syria whom she deserted to become Felix's third wife. She would have been about twenty years of age at the time.

They listen to Paul's message of "faith in Jesus Christ." Luke offers a triadic summary of the salient points at which the interest of even a kindly disposed wordling turns to fright as his life is brought under judgment. "Justice" is the attribute of God to be manifested in "the judgment to come" (cf. 17:31). The theme is expanded in the discourse to Agrippa (26:23). That Paul is not released Luke ascribes to the venality that was a well-known feature of provincial administrators, but also to the desire of Felix to do a favour to the Jews as his administration draws to a close.

PAUL APPEALS TO CAESAR. 25:1-12.

25 Now when Festus had come into his province, after three days he went up to Jerusalem from Caesarea. [2]And the chief priests and the principal men of the Jews informed him against Paul; and they urged him, [3]asking as a favour to have the man sent to Jerusalem, planning an ambush to kill him on the way. [4]Festus replied that Paul was being kept at Caesarea, and that he himself intended to go there shortly. [5]"So," said he, "let the men of authority among you go down with me, and if there is anything wrong about the man, let them accuse him."

[6]When he had stayed among them not more than eight or ten days, he went down to Caesarea; and the next day he took his seat on the tribunal and ordered Paul to be brought. [7]And when he had come, the Jews who had gone down from Jerusalem stood about him, bringing against him many serious charges which they could not prove.

> [8]Paul said in his defence, "Neither against the law of the Jews, nor against the temple, nor against Caesar have I offended at all." [9]But Festus, wishing to do the Jews a favour, said to Paul, "Do you wish to go up to Jerusalem, and there be tried on these charges before me?" [10]But Paul said, "I am standing before Caesar's tribunal, where I ought to be tried; to the Jews I have done no wrong, as you know very well.[11]If then I am a wrongdoer, and have committed anything for which I deserve to die, I do not seek to escape death; but if there is nothing in their charges against me, no one can give me up to them. I appeal to Caesar." [12]Then Festus, when he had conferred with his council, answered, "You have appealed to Caesar; to Caesar you shall go."

The continuing controversy, briefly interrupted by vv.24-27, continues before the new governor Festus. Festus was Roman procurator from A.D. 60-62. What little is known of him agrees with Luke's picture of an honourable man and a businesslike administrator. "The high priests and principal men of the Jews" resume their attack on Paul and renew plans to do away with him. Festus avoids their request to transfer Paul to Jerusalem and invites them to prefer charges against Paul in Caesarea.

The trial scene does not go into the details of charges Luke has already listed (24:5-6). Luke simply shows that they are groundless. No proof can be adduced (v.7). Paul makes a blanket protestation of innocence, which includes an element so far unheard since it extends beyond crimes that are a breach of Jewish law to crimes against Caesar (v.8). What advances the story is the govenor's request that Paul be transferred from Caesarea to his court in Jerusalem, which provokes another protestation of innocence on Paul's part and an appeal to Caesar to ensure that nobody "will make a gift of him" to the Jews. Festus confers with his council and Paul's request is granted.

FESTUS AND AGRIPPA. "CERTAIN POINTS OF DISPUTE." 25:13-22.

> [13]Now when some days had passed, Agrippa the king and Bernice arrived at Caesarea to welcome Festus. [14]And as they stayed there many days, Festus laid Paul's case before the king, saying, "There is a man left prisoner by Felix; [15]and when I was at Jerusalem, the chief priests and the elders of the Jews gave information about him, asking for sentence against him. [16]I answered them that it was not the custom of the Romans to give up any one before the accused met the accusers face to face, and had opportunity to make his defence concerning the charge laid against him. [17]When therefore they came together here, I made no delay, but on the next day took my seat on the tribunal and ordered the man to be brought in. [18]When the accusers stood up, they brought no charge in his case of such evils as I supposed; [19]but they had certain points of dispute with him about their own superstition and about one Jesus, who was dead, but whom Paul asserted to be alive. [20]Being at a loss how to investigate these questions, I asked whether he wished to go to Jerusalem and be tried there regarding them. [21]But when Paul had appealed to be kept in custody for the decision of the emperor, I commanded him to be held until I could send him to Caesar." [22]And Agrippa said to Festus, "I should like to hear the man myself." "Tomorrow," said he, "you shall hear him."

Prior to the climactic discourse which concludes the section comes an interlude which brings together the Roman governor and the last of the Jewish kings. Herod Agrippa II, great-grandson of Herod the Great and son of Herod Agrippa I whose death Luke has described in 12:20-23, had been brought up in Rome. His territory did not include Judea, which had been under direct Roman rule since 6 A.D. (with the exception of the last three years of his father's reign), but he was acknowledged as superintendent of the Temple with the right to nominate and depose the high priest. His sister Bernice cut a swathe through the history of her times as not the least enterprising of her well-known family. She had been living with her brother, since the death of her uncle and first husband, in a relationship publicly branded as incestuous, before a second marriage to the king of Cilicia after which she became the mistress of Titus. The scene offers no new information; the discourse of Festus puts the dilemma of a Roman governor to a man of experience in matters of Jewish religion as well as Roman law. It re-states Paul's innocence (v.8) and offers the judgment of a Roman official that the controversy between Paul and the Jews concerns "their own superstition and one Jesus who is dead, but whom Paul asserts to be alive" (v.19). Agrippa's eagerness to see Paul is like that of Herod Antipas to see Jesus (Lk 9:9; 23:8). The scene is set for Paul's appearance before "governors and kings."

PAUL'S DEFENCE BEFORE AGRIPPA. 25:23 - 26:32.

> [23]So on the morrow Agrippa and Bernice came with great pomp, and they entered the audience hall with the military tribunes and the prominent men of the city. Then by command of Festus Paul was brought in. [24]And Festus said, "King Agrippa and all who are present with us, you see this man about whom the whole Jewish people petitioned me, both at Jerusalem and here, shouting that he ought not to live any longer. [25]But I found that he had done nothing deserving death; and as he himself appealed to the emperor, I decided to send him. [26]But I have nothing definite to write to my lord about him. Therefore I have brought him before you, and, especially before you, King Agrippa, that, after we have examined him, I may have something to write. [27]For it seems to me unreasonable, in sending a prisoner, not to indicate the charges against him."

26 Agrippa said to Paul, "You have permission to speak for yourself." Then Paul stretched out his hand and made his defence:

[2]"I think myself fortunate that it is before you, King Agrippa, I am to make my defence today against all the accusations of the Jews, [3]because you are especially familiar with all customs and controversies of the Jews; therefore I beg you to listen to me patiently.

[4]"My manner of life from my youth, spent from the beginning among my own nation and at Jerusalem, is known by all the Jews. [5]They have known for a long time, if they are willing to testify, that according to the strictest party of our religion I have lived as a Pharisee. [6]And now I stand here on trial for hope in the promise made by God to our fathers, [7]to which our twelve tribes hope to attain, as they earnestly worship night and day. And for this hope I am accused by Jews, O king! [8]Why is it thought incredible by any of you that God raises the dead?

[9]"I myself was convinced that I ought to do many things in opposing the name of Jesus of Nazareth. [10]And I did so in Jerusalem; I not only shut up many of the saints in prison, by authority from the chief priests, but when they were put to death I cast my vote against them. [11]And I punished them often in all the synagogues and tried to make them blaspheme; and in raging fury against them, I persecuted them even to foreign cities.

[12]"Thus I journeyed to Damascus with the authority and commission of the chief priests. [13]At midday, O king, I saw on the way a light from heaven, brighter than the sun, shining round me and those who journeyed with me. [14]And when we had all fallen to the ground, I heard a voice saying to me in the Hebrew language, 'Saul, Saul, why to you persecute me? It hurts you to kick against the goads.' [15]And I said, 'Who are you, Lord?' And the Lord said, 'I am Jesus whom you are persecuting. [16]But rise and stand upon your feet; for I have appeared to you for this purpose, to appoint you to serve and bear witness

to the things in which you have seen me and to those in which I will appear to you, [17]delivering you from the people and from the Gentiles—to whom I send you [18]to open their eyes, that they may turn from darkness to light and from the power of Satan to God, that they may receive forgiveness of sins and a place among those who are sanctified by faith in me.'

[19]"Wherefore, O King Agrippa, I was not disobedient to the heavenly vision, [20]but declared first to those at Damascus, then at Jerusalem and throughout all the country of Judea, and also to the Gentiles, that they should repent and turn to God and perform deeds worthy of their repentance. [21]For this reason the Jews seized me in the temple and tried to kill me. [22]To this day I have had the help that comes from God, and so I stand here testifying both to small and great, saying nothing but what the prophets and Moses said would come to pass; [23]that the Christ must suffer, and that, by being the first to rise from the dead, he would proclaim light both to the people and to the Gentiles."

[24]And as he thus made his defence, Festus said with a loud voice, "Paul, you are mad; your great learning is turning you mad." [25]But Paul said, "I am not mad, most excellent Festus, but I am speaking the sober truth. [26]For the king knows about these things, and to him I speak freely; for I am persuaded that none of these things has escaped his notice, for this was not done in a corner. [27]King Agrippa, do you believe the prophets? I know that you believe." [28]And Agrippa said to Paul, "In a short time you think to make me a Christian!" [29]And Paul said, "Whether short or long, I would to God that not only you but also all who hear me this day might become such as I am—except for these chains."

[30]Then the king rose, and the governor and Bernice and those who were sitting with them; [31]and when they had withdrawn, they said to one another, "This man is doing nothing to deserve death or imprisonment."

> [32]And Agrippa said to Festus, "This man could have been set free if he had not appealed to Caesar."

Chapters 22-26 come to a climax and conclusion in Paul's final self-defence against the charges of his opponents, for which all that has preceded can be seen as preparation. It is significant that "the Jews" now disappear from the scene. In his last appearance in the Jewish world Paul justifies himself and Christianity in the presence of a Jewish king, but before a mainly pagan audience, and with a careful turn of Greek phrase in a discourse that places a Greek proverb on the lips of the risen Christ. There is no more mention of the desecration of the Temple, the discourse concentrates on the central issues of the continuity of Christianity with Judaism and the origin of the mission of Paul to the pagans and, of course, of the Church in Luke's own time.

The reader is already more than familiar with the charges Paul is meeting and the line of argument he adopts. The repetitions of the section have been calculated to achieve precisely this effect. What remains is a final elaboration which permits Luke to restate central points of the message of his two volumes and suggest more clearly their application to the changed world of his reader. Again it is clear that much of the scene is due to the work of Luke. The reason Festus alleges for convoking the session (v.26) is hardly convincing in view of the information already available to him. The material concerning Paul's conversion has already been used twice before by Luke (9:1-19; 22:3-16); some differences in detail can be seen as simply literary variation or expansion; other statements are theological conceptions dear to Luke.

In a very impressive ceremonial setting, Agrippa and Bernice come "with great pomp" and an entourage including civic and military dignitaries. Festus' introductory words mark out a very real opposition between the view of "the whole Jewish people" and the judgment of the Roman governor on the innocence of Paul (vv.24-25).

Paul's speech commences with the customary oratorical gestures, both manual (v.1) and verbal (vv.2-3). He begins the familiar recitation. The Jewishness of his earlier way of life is common knowledge, lived, indeed, "according to the strictest sect of our religion" (v.5). The issue that brings him to trial is as simple as the heart of the Jewish religion, "the hope in the promise made by God to our fathers," the object of Israel's daily pious aspiration. The reader knows that this hope is the resurrection of the dead (23:6). How absurd for Jews to refuse to believe in it!

The picture of Paul's activity as persecutor (vv.10-11) is painted in blacker colours than before (cf. 8:3; 22:4); Paul has participated in trials which condemned Christians to death. The story of his conversions (vv.12-18) differs in details from the two previous versions. The proverb addressed to Paul by the risen Jesus is unknown in Jewish literature but a commonplace in the Hellenistic world; it expresses the impossibility of opposing the power of Jesus and applies not only to Paul's persecuting activity but to the mission that is to be entrusted to him. Ananias does not appear at all; Paul's call as an apostle comes direct from the risen Christ. It is an appointment as "servant," one of those "servants of the word" from whom Luke says his two volumes derive (cf. Lk 1:2), and as "witness," hence a peer of the original "witnesses" (cf. Acts 1:8), but to the risen Lord whom he has encountered in this vision and will encounter in others to come.

Allusions to the vocations of Ezechiel (Ezek 2:1), Jeremiah (Jer 1:5-8), and second Isaiah (Is 42:7,16) show that in his mission both to Jews and Gentiles he will enjoy God's protection but also that he is a legitimate successor of those Jewish prophets who had articulated the form taken by God's "promise to our fathers," in their particular times. He is to "open their eyes," continuing the mission of Jesus (Lk 4:18). To "turn them back" (cf. Lk 1:17; Acts 3:19; 14:15), and "forgiveness of sins" (Lk 1:77; 24:27; Acts 2:38; 5:31), are favourite Lucan conceptions. By Paul's activity Jews and Gentiles alike will be brought to share the inheritance promised by God to Abraham and already obtained by those who have faith in Christ.

Paul outlines his subsequent career (vv.19-23) in fidelity to his heavenly commission. To Jews and Gentiles he has proclaimed "repentance and turning back to God." Like John the Baptist he has called for "deeds worthy of repentance" (cf. Lk 3:8). And it is for this preaching of repentance and conversion to Jews and Gentiles that he was seized by the Jews. Other issues are dropped; the heart of the controversy between Jews and Christians is revealed. The final phrase reveals how Luke saw the Jewish hope of the resurrection of the dead fulfilled. The message of Paul, a prophet himself, is in complete accord with the prophets and Moses in his proclamation of a Messiah who "had to suffer." The new insight into the Scriptures they share with the Jews makes clear this paradoxical aspect of God's plan that lies revealed in them. Jesus' death was necessary to inaugurate the era of the resurrection by himself first rising from the dead so as to "proclaim light to the people and the Gentiles" in the mission of the witnesses he commissioned.

Two interchanges follow, permitting Luke to contrast the response of the Roman governor, incapable of appreciating the theological issues dividing Paul and the Jews and ascribing Paul's performance to religious frenzy, and the Jewish king, versed in the Scriptures and familiar with the hopes of Israel, who avoids committing himself with an ambiguous remark. The audience breaks up. The king, the governor and his advisers agree on Paul's innocence. Were it not for Paul's appeal to Caesar which has forced Festus' hand he could go free.

At the end of this section Paul's witness in Jerusalem is complete. He has done all he possibly could to show his solidarity with James and the Jewish Christians - indeed his bending over backward to do so became the occasion for his imprisonment. Against official Judaism he has argued that Christianity's central belief is the fulfilment of the heart of the Jewish religion particularly as practised by the Pharisees. The real issue against him has been revealed as the mission to the Gentiles and he has testified that this mission orginated in an express divine initiative, an encounter with the Messiah, the risen Jesus who commissioned him as another prophet to preach "light to the nations."

When Luke wrote, Paul's arguments with official Judaism were a matter of past history. His story answered the questions of a later generation of Christians about their origins in Judaism and explained the reasons for the differences between themselves and the people of whom Jesus was born. It provided responses to the complaints still being made about them by the Jews to Roman authorities. From the very beginning Roman officials had attested the Christians innocent of any crime against the empire.

Nor were their origins obscure, "things done in a corner." Luke has systematically shown Christianity not only in its relations with Judaism, but in its relations with the Roman empire, into which Jesus was born, under the guidance of whose officials its early history took place, and to which his readers were called in their generation to continue the "witness" exemplified in the great hero of the past.

VOYAGE AND SHIPWRECK.
27:1-44.

> **27** And when it was decided that we should sail for Italy, they delivered Paul and some other prisoners to a centurion of the Augustan Cohort, named Julius. [2]And embarking in a ship of Adramyttium, which was about to sail to the ports along the coast of Asia, we put to sea, accompanied by Aristarchus, a Macedonian from Thessalonica. [3]The next day we put in at Sidon; and Julius treated Paul kindly, and gave him leave to go to his friends and be cared for. [4]And putting to sea from there we sailed under the lee of Cyprus, because the winds were against us. [5]And when we had sailed across the

sea which is off Cilicia and Pamphylia, we came to Myra in Lycia. [6]There the centurion found a ship of Alexandria sailing for Italy, and put us on board. [7]We sailed slowly for a number of days, and arrived with difficulty off Cnidus, and as the wind did not allow us to go on, we sailed under the lee of Crete off Salmone. [8]Coasting along it with difficulty, we came to a place called Fair Havens, near which was the city of Lasea.

[9]As much time had been lost, and the voyage was already dangerous because the fast had already gone by, Paul advised them, [10]saying, "Sirs, I perceive that the voyage will be with injury and much loss, not only of the cargo and the ship, but also of our lives." [11]But the centurion paid more attention to the captain and to the owner of the ship than to what Paul said. [12]And because the harbour was not suitable to winter in, the majority advised to put to sea from there, on the chance that somehow they could reach Phoenix, a harbour of Crete, looking northeast and southeast, and winter there.

[13]And when the south wind blew gently, supposing that they had obtained their purpose, they weighed anchor and sailed along Crete, close inshore. [14]But soon a tempestuous wind, called the northeaster, struck down from the land; [15] and when the ship was caught and could not face the wind, we gave way to it and were driven. [16]And running under the lee of a small island called Cauda, we managed with difficulty to secure the boat; [17]after hoisting it up, they took measures to undergird the ship; then, fearing that they should run on the Syrtis, they lowered the gear, and so were driven. [18]As we were violently storm-tossed, they began next day to throw the cargo overboard; [19]and the third day they cast out with their own hands the tackle of the ship. [20]And when neither sun nor stars appeared for many a day, and no small tempest lay on us, all hope of our being saved was at last abandoned.

[21]As they had been long without food, Paul then came forward among them and said, "Men, you should have listened to me, and should not have set sail from Crete and incurred this injury and loss. [22]I now bid you take heart;for there will be no loss of life among you, but only of the ship. [23]For this very night there stood by me an angel of the God to whom I belong and whom I worship, [24]and he said, 'Do not be afraid, Paul; you must stand before Caesar; and lo, God has granted you all those who sail with you.' [25]So take heart, men, for I have faith in God that it will be exactly as I have been told. [26]But we shall have to run on some island."

[27]When the fourteenth night had come, as we were drifting across the sea of Adria, about midnight the sailors suspected that they were nearing land. [28]So they sounded and found twenty fathoms; a little father on they sounded again and found fifteen fathoms. [29]And fearing that we might run on the rocks, they let out four anchors from the stern, and prayed for day to come. [30]And as the sailors were seeking to escape from the ship, and had lowered the boat into the sea, under pretence of laying out anchors from the bow, [31]Paul said to the centurion and the soldiers, "Unless these men stay in the ship, you cannot be saved." [32]Then the soldiers cut away the ropes of the boat, and let it go.

[33]As day was about to dawn, Paul urged them all to take some food, saying, "Today is the fourteenth day that you have continued in suspense and without food, having taken nothing. [34]Therefore I urge you to take some food; it will give you strength, since not a hair is to perish from the head of any of you." [35]And when he had said this, he took bread, and giving thanks to God in the presence of all he broke it and began to eat. [36]Then they all were encouraged and ate some food themselves. [37](We were in all two hundred and seventy-six persons in the ship.) [38]And when they had eaten enough, they

lightened the ship, throwing out the wheat into the sea. [39]Now when it was day, they did not recognise the land, but they noticed a bay with a beach, on which they planned if possible to bring the ship ashore. [40]So they cast off the anchors and left them in the sea, at the same time loosening the ropes that tied the rudders; then hoisting the foresail to the wind they made for the beach. [41]But striking a shoal they ran the vessel aground; the bow stuck and remained immovable, and the stern was broken up by the surf. [42]The soldiers' plan was to kill the prisoners, lest any should swim away and escape; [43]but the centurion, wishing to save Paul, kept them from carrying out their purpose. He ordered those who could swim to throw themselves overboard first and make for the land, [44]and the rest on planks or on pieces of the ship. And so it was that all escaped to land.

The last two chapters complete the programme Luke has marked out from his opening verses. Paul's journey to Rome completes not only the programme of the apostle's career (of which the reader has already twice been reminded in 19:21; 23:11), but also the programme of Luke's second volume, the spread of the witness to Christ "from Jerusalem to the ends of the earth" (1:8). Paul "must" indeed visit Rome, but in circumstances entirely different from those he would have planned, for it is not Paul's plan but God's which is being fulfilled. Despite human plans that end in shipwreck (27:11-22), God's care brings Paul and his fellow travellers to safety and preserves him immune from harm to "bear witness at Rome."

Paul's own words show that he was no stranger to such "dangers at sea" as Luke describes. "Three times have I been shipwrecked, a night and a day I have been adrift at sea" (2 Cor 11:25). Where Luke obtained the material for this chapter, however, remains a matter of dispute. Paul appears at decisive moments of the story, admittedly, but the sections in which he does (vv.9-11, 21-26; 33-36,43) can easily be removed from the narrative and their exclusion leaves a story of admirable, if sometimes confusing, nautical detail which differs little from stories of journeys and shipwrecks common in travel novels of the Hellenistic world. Scholars differ on the question of Luke's sources, debating whether he has simply taken over some such account and inserted suitable interventions of Paul, or whether he is using an account of one of Paul's companions of the voyage edited and arranged in his own way. The "We" that appear would thus emphasize the eye-witness character of his story without identifying his source.

Sailing in the Mediterranean was a risky business at any time after the middle of September. From the middle of November travel by ship practically ceased until the return of the westerly winds at the beginning of spring in early March. Paul accompanied by Aristarchus (19:29), sets out with other prisoners. As usual the Roman officer treats him with kindness and he visits the Christian community at Sidon (v.3). Small vessels were generally obliged to hug the shore line but adverse winds forced them to adopt a north-westerly course to Myra in Lycia. Of the possible ways of reaching Rome from there the centurion chooses to embark his prisoners on an Egyptian freighter which slowly works its way to the Port called "Fair Havens" on Crete.

Paul's first intervention comes at vv.9-10. It is hardly surprising that the captain, the owner of the ship, and the majority of the seamen pay little attention; the counsels of the experts prevail. All seems to go well as they set sail for Phoenix, a better harbour one day's sailing away, then the wind veers right round and drives violently from the northwest. Unable to keep the bow to the waves they are obliged to run before the wind, profiting by a lull as they pass on the lee side of the small island of Cauda to get the ship's dinghy aboard and taking action to strengthen the hull against the violence of the waves. Then, afraid of being driven on the sand-banks extending well out into the Gulf of Syrte west of Cyrenaica, a sea-anchor is dragged behind the vessel, cargo and ship's tackle are thrown overboard.

Paul's next intervention is placed at the moment of direct necessity (vv.21-26) with the ship being driven by the tempest, all possibility of navigation gone, their position unknown, in short "when all hope of our being saved was at last abandoned." Paul's words of encouragement bear the imprint of Luke's thinking and language. God's messenger has assured Paul that he "must stand before Caesar" and that the others will be saved because of him. He predicts that they will strike an island - a very faint possibility in the open sea between Crete, Africa and Sicily.

The immediate sequence shows this prophecy fulfilled. Paul again takes the initiative and directs the centurion (v.31) to take action in circumstances difficult to explain, for the sailors who seek to escape (v.30) would be far safer on board ship riding offshore at anchor than committing themselves to a landing on an unknown coast in a small boat in a heavy sea. Paul again encourages them (v.35-36) to strengthen themselves for what lies ahead. His gesture (v.35) is described in terms parallel to that of Jesus at the Last Supper (Lk 22:19); the text lacks only the phrase "he gave it to them." In this extremity Paul engages in the characteristic Christian "breaking of bread" (2:42; 20:7); the others are thus encouraged to take food themselves.

The action of the centurion (v.32) has left them without a dinghy and obliged them to steer for the shore. They cut away the anchors and bring the rudders into action to steer for the bay, hoist the small foresail to ensure sufficient speed for steering, and strike a shoal at the mouth of the bay. The soldiers propose to kill their prisoners since loss of the captive one was guarding could involve a guard in the loss of his own life, but the centurion countermands this "plan" (v.43). As Paul has prophesied, all are saved.

MALTA.
28:1-10.

28 After we had escaped, we then learned that the island was called Malta. [2]And the natives showed us unusual kindness, for they kindled a fire and welcomed us all, because it had begun to rain and was cold. [3]Paul had gathered a bundle of sticks and put them on the fire, when a viper came out because of the heat and fastened on his hand. [4]When the natives saw the creature hanging from his hand, they said to one another, "No doubt this man is a murderer. Though he has escaped from the sea, justice has not allowed him to live." [5]He, however, shook off the creature into the fire and suffered no harm. [6]They waited, expecting him to swell up or suddenly fall down dead; but when they had waited a long time and saw no misfortune come to him, they changed their minds and said that he was a god.

[7]Now in the neighbourhood of that place were lands belonging to the chief man of the island, named Publius, who received us and entertained us hospitably for three days. [8]It happened that the father of Publius lay sick with fever and dysentery; and Paul visited him and prayed, and putting his hands on him healed him. [9]And when this had taken place, the rest of the people on the island who had diseases also came and were cured. [10]They presented many gifts to us; and when we sailed, they put on board whatever we needed.

The story of the stay at Malta is made up of two miracle stories. For the time being the centurion disappears, as in fact do all the other passengers except those referred to by the "we." Contrary to all expectation the "barbarians" show the castaways an "unusual kindness." The miracles are the last of the "signs and wonders" Luke is to relate. The first illustrates God's protection of Paul, saved from shipwreck only to be bitten by a viper. The apostle benefits from the power given by Jesus to his heralds (Lk 10:19; cf. Mk 16:18), the miracle brings about in the superstitious pagans an attitude to Paul comparable to that of the Lycaonians (cf. 14:11). The second miracle happens in response to the warm hospitality of "the chief man of the island" and is followed by a generalising summary (v.9).

"AND SO WE CAME TO ROME." 28:11-16.

> [11]After three months we set sail in a ship which had wintered in the island, a ship of Alexandria, with the Twin Brothers as figurehead. [12]Putting in at Syracuse, we stayed there for three days. [13]And from there we made a circuit and arrived at Rhegium; and after one day a south wind sprang up, and on the second day we came to Puteoli. [14]There we found brethren, and were invited to stay with them for seven days. And so we came to Rome. [15]And the brethren there, when they heard of us, came as far as the Forum of Appius and Three Taverns to meet us. On seeing them Paul thanked God and took courage. [16]And when we came into Rome, Paul was allowed to stay by himself, with the soldier that guarded him.

The final stages of the journey are accomplished. Probably in early February the three-month stay in Malta came to a close. On an Alexandrian ship bearing the effigy of Castor and Pollux, the two sone of Zeus and patrons of pagan sailors, the apostle of the one true God travels from Malta to Syracuse and thence to Rhegium and Puteoli on the Gulf of Naples, to be greeted by the Christian community there. Luke makes Paul's arrival in Rome something of a triumphant procession. He is greeted at two of the main stopping places, the Forum of Appius some forty miles from Rome and the Three Taverns about ten miles closer, by members of the Christian community of Rome, a welcome at which "Paul thanked God and took courage." The final verse alone reminds us of his captive state.

FINALE. "THE SALVATION OF GOD SENT TO THE GENTILES." 28:17-31.

[17]After three days he called together the local leaders of the Jews; and when they had gathered, he said to them, "Brethren, though I had done nothing against the people or the customs of our fathers, yet I was delivered prisoner from Jerusalem into the hands of the Romans. [18]When they had examined me, they wished to set me at liberty, because there was no reason for the death penalty in my case. [19]But when the Jews objected, I was compelled to appeal to Caesar—though I had no charge to bring against my nation. [20]For this reason therefore I have asked to see you and speak with you, since it is because of the hope of Israel that I am bound with this chain." [21]And they had said to him, "We have received no letters from Judea about you, and none of the brethren coming here has reported or spoken any evil about you. [22]But we desire to hear from you what your views are; for with regard to this sect we know that everywhere it is spoken against."

[23]When they had appointed a day for him, they came to him at his lodging in great numbers. And he expounded the matter to them from morning till evening, testifying to the kingdom of God and trying to convince them about Jesus both from the law of Moses and from the prophets. [24]And some were convinced by what he said, while others disbelieved. [25]So, as they disagreed among themselves, they departed, after Paul had made one statement: "The Holy Spirit was right in saying to your fathers through Isaiah the prophet:

[26]'Go to this people, and say,
You shall indeed hear but never understand,
and you shall indeed see but never perceive.
[27]For this people's heart has grown dull,

and their ears are heavy of hearing,
and their eyes they have closed;
lest they should perceive with their eyes,
and hear with their ears,
and understand with their heart,
and turn for me to heal them.'

[28]Let it be known to you then that this salvation of God has been sent to the Gentiles; they will listen."

[30]And he lived there two whole years at his own expense, and welcomed all who came to him, [31]preaching the kingdom of God and teaching about the Lord Jesus Christ quite openly and unhindered.

"And so we came to Rome." The goal of the apostle's long journey is attained, yet Luke's picture is not complete with his arrival at "the ends of the earth." Two scenes showing Paul's relations with the Jewish community in Rome (vv.17-22, 23-28) precede the epilogue (vv.30-31). The two scenes are systematically arranged. Paul "convokes" the local Jewish leaders and puts his case to them. Paul's discourse (vv.17-20) is a very abbreviated presentation, understandable only to someone familiar with the earlier stories of his self-defence in Jerusalem. It is tailored diplomatically to Paul's audience; his statement that he "was delivered prisoner from Jerusalem into the hands of the Romans" (v.17), though it underscores the similarity of his fate to that of Jesus (Lk 24:7), does scant justice to the fact that he owed his life to the Romans. Though compelled to appeal to Caesar "when the Jews objected," he is well disposed towards his people, in fact "it is because of the hope of Israel that I am bound with this chain" (v.20). The remark of the Jewish leaders (v.22) states the realities of Luke's time rather than those of Paul, and the apostle's words (vv.17-18) present the outlines of the Christian response.

Luke's two volumes conclude in parallel fashion. His first volume closes with a solemn declaration of the risen

Christ and a Lucan epilogue (Lk 24:44-49, 59-63), his second with a declaration of Paul (vv.25-28) and an epilogue of his own construction. At the end of the first volume the Risen Christ opens the minds of his disciples to the understanding of the Scriptures to enable them to read there the mystery of his death and resurrection and the mission to all nations. He then commissions them as his witnesses. At the end of Acts, Paul is in Rome fulfilling this commission in the light of that understanding, "witnessing to the kingdom of God and persuading them about Jesus from the law of Moses and the prophets." His testimony is as divisive in its turn as the person and message of Jesus in his time (Lk 2:34-35; 4:20-30). Luke notes that "some were persuaded" (v.24) but Paul's declaration shows that the emphasis falls rather on the unbelief of the others.

The quotation from Isaiah 6:9-10 (vv.26-27) comes from the vocation of the prophet. It is a passage in which Christians well before Luke had found, if not an explanation for the fact that few of Jesus' fellows had accepted his message, then at least an intimation that in his rejection by his people he was following in the footsteps of Israel's own prophets and that somehow the events of the life of Jesus and the continuing history of the mission to the Jews formed a part of God's "plan." Paul's mission is likened to that of Jesus and Isaiah whose preaching "to this people" was intended as a light to illumine their darkness but which finally blinded a people who would not understand their need for conversion. Paul's last words (v.28) take us back to the beginning of Luke's first volume in the proclamation of the prophet Simeon and the message of John the Baptist (Lk 2:30; 3:4-6). The "salvation" which, according to the prophet (Is 40:3) must be proclaimed "to all flesh," has been sent to the Gentiles because of Israel's refusal.

This is the third time Paul pronounces the judgment that has come on Israel (cf. 13:46; 18:6). At the close of Luke's work it has a definitive ring. This was the situation as Luke knew it in his time. The Church he knew was predominantly

Gentile. Jewish in its origins, its message no longer was accepted by the Jews. Events since the time of Paul, especially the ruin of Jerusalem and the Temple, had not softened but hardened antagonism between Judaism, especially official Judaism, and Christianity. These sad facts of its history Luke knew and wrote into his story, not simply as a summary of the past but as warning of future possibilities for the People of Yahweh he knew. The same pattern of grace offered and grace refused, of conflict and triumph, of death and resurrection would be repeated in the church's experience. As history unfolded, the pattern would touch different peoples in different cultures, but the work of the Spirit would continue "unhindered" on its surprising way to completion.

The epilogue (vv.30-31) summarizes Paul's two-year imprisonment in Rome. The "prisoner of Jesus Christ" continues in his missionary work. The epilogue paints him in a characteristic pose that captures the whole of his career "preaching the kingdom of God and teaching boldly about the Lord Jesus," profiting from the occasion offered by his Roman captors.

Luke's second volume comes to an abrupt conclusion. With Paul's preaching in Rome he has fulfilled his purpose; the command of the risen Lord has been fulfilled. Luke's audience knew about the death of Paul just as it knew that Christianity reached Rome before him. His career illustrated the dynamism of the Gospel. It invites Theophilus and others after him to take their part in the continuing action.

FURTHER READING

The reader who has commenced the study of Acts with this volume or one of comparable range and is seeking greater depth or more detailed information can consult, as a next step, the commentaries on Acts in one or other of the standard modern one-volume commentaries on the Bible. Two of the better known are:

Dillon, R.J., & Fitzmyer, J.A., "Acts of the Apostles" in *The Jerome Biblical Commentary* (eds. R.E. Brown, J.A. Fitzmyer, R.E. Murphy) London: Chapman, 1968, 2:165-214.

Lampe, G.W.H., "Acts, in *Peake's Commentary on the Bible* (eds. M. Black, H.H. Rowley) London: Nelson, 1964, 882-926.

There are comprehensive treatments of such matters as authorship and date, language and style, sources, audience and historical value in standard works of introduction to the New Testament, such as

Cerfaux, L., "The Acts of the Apostles" in *Introduction to the New Testament* (eds. A. Robert, A. Feuillet) New York: Desclee, 1965, 328-368.

Kummel, W. G., *Introduction to the New Testament*, New York: Abingdon, Rev. Ed., 1973, 151-188.

Many of the literary aspects of the work of Luke have been studied in

Cadbury, H.J., *The Style and Literary Method of Luke* Cambridge: Harvard University Press, 1920, reprinted in 1969 by Kraus Reprint Co.

Only the first part of this treatment of Luke as "an individual author of the Hellenistic age," pp. 1-72, concerns itself with Acts. The same author's

The Making of Luke-Acts New York: Macmillan, 1927, is a much more extensive treatment, particularly Part 2, "The Common Method," 113-209, and Part 3, "The

Personality of the Author," 113-296. The second edition (London: S.P.C.K., 1958, reprinted in 1961) testifies to its continuing value.

For the interplay of literary medium and Gospel message more recent writers should be consulted, especially

Beardslee, W.A. *Literary Criticism of the New Testament*, Philadelphia: Fortress, 1970.

A series of essays which concentrate on the religious function of the narrative. Particularly useful are Chapter 4, "History as a Form," 42-52, and Chapter 7, "Literary Criticism and Theological Understanding," 75-83.

Wilder, A.N., *Early Christian Rhetoric. The Language of the Gospel*, Cambridge: Harvard University Press, 1976.

Written to take account of some of the most recent developments in the specifically "literary" and rhetorical aspects of New Testament study. Chapter 4, "The Story," 55-70, is of special interest.

Two books could be named as central in the approach to Acts that dominates most recent research. They have become co-ordinates with respect to which other authors mark out their positions.

Conzelmann, H., *The Theology of St. Luke*, New York: Harper & Row, 1960.

This is a seminal work which both signalled the advent of Redaction Criticism and established Luke as a theologian in his own right.

Haenchen, E., *The Acts of the Apostle. A Commentary*. Philadelphia: Westminister, 1971.

The major recent commentary available in English. Great detail, a mastery of past authors, insistent pursuit of the intention of Luke in details and arrangement of episodes.

For the history of the early Church in New Testament times, the following can be consulted:

Brown, R.E., Donfried, K.P., Reumann, J. (eds.), *Peter in the New Testament.* Augsburg: Minneapolis and New York: Paulist, 1973.

The sub-title indicates some of its special interest, "A Collaborative Assessment by Protestant and Roman Catholic Scholars." A detailed study of the evidence, roughly in chronological order. Chapter 2, "Presuppositions for the Study," Chapter 3, "Peter in the Pauline Letters" and Chapter 4, "Peter in the Books of Acts," 23-56, are of immediate relevance.

Conzelmann, H. *History of Primitive Christianity.* New York: Abingdon, 1972.

Goppelt, L., *Apostolic and Post-Apostolic Times*, New York: Harper & Row, 1970.

Perrin, N., *The New Testament. An Introduction.* New York: Harcourt, Brace, Jovanovich, 1974.

Distinct in style and scope from works like Kummel. Of particular interest are Chapter 3, "A Theological History of Early Christianity," 39-63, and Chapter 9, "The Gospel of Luke and the Acts of the Apostles" 195-219.

Two volumes of essays by international groups of scholars may serve to indicate the main concerns in scholarly research into Luke-Acts in the past two decades.

Gasque, W.W., & Martin, R.P., (eds.) *Apostolic History and the Gospel. Biblical and Historical Essays.* Exeter: Paternoster, 1970.

The first nine essays are devoted to the language, theology, history, purpose and archaeology of Acts.

Keck, L., & Martin, R.P. (eds.), *Studies in Luke-Acts.* Nashville: Abingdon, 1966.

Essays on the style of Acts, its text, theological interpretation, historical background and position in early Christianity.

Among the multitude of monographs three are singled out because of the importance of the subject they treat

Dupont, J., *The Sources of Acts. The Present Position.* London: Darton, Longman & Todd, 1964.

The only work available in English of the extensive work of the most distinguished Roman Catholic scholar in the field. A guide through the thickets of past theories.

Lindars, B., *New Testament Apologetic. The Doctrinal Significance of the Old Testament Quotations.* London: S.C.M., 1961.

On the development of the early Church's understanding of the Scriptures and the factors that stimulated it.

Wilson, S.G., *The Gentiles and the Gentile Mission in Luke-Acts.* Cambridge University Press, 1973.

As a bibliographical aid

Mattill, A.J., & M.B., *A Classified Bibliography of Literature on the Acts of the Apostles.* Leiden: Brill, 1966.

For studies published prior to 1961.